Annuities, Mutual Funds & Life Insurance

as investment products

the INSTITUTE of financial education
111 EAST WACKER DRIVE/CHICAGO, ILLINOIS 60601

ISBN 0-912857-46-3
Library of Congress Catalog Card Number: 88-81299

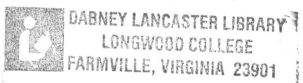

CONTENTS

PREFACE

In only a few years, a basic knowledge of annuities, mutual funds, and life insurance has become essential for managers and customer contact staff—more than just "nice to know." As savings institutions market these products more widely, this need continues to expand.

Savings institution professionals who have recognized this need for themselves or their staff have, until now, faced a problem. It has been easy to find a mass of technical material about these products. Many of these books, however, are much more procedural and legalistic than readers want or need. Few books contain the particular group of investment alternatives that savings institutions are most likely to add to their product lines. Until this publication, savings institution personnel could not rely on one source to provide them with information on these nontraditional products in a concise format.

Annuities, Mutual Funds and Life Insurance as Investment Products presents major features and benefits of these products in a clear, readable manner. The subject matter can be easily absorbed even by those with little or no previous knowledge of each type of investment. Furthermore, each product is also considered from the customer's point of view. With this information, staff members can anticipate customer questions and concerns. In addition, an important final section describes the steps in conducting a successful selling interview.

We hope that this book serves readers in several ways. It is a concise reference book for managers and staff throughout the savings institution. It is an overview for institutions that are considering adding these products and for institutions that do not sell these products but have competitors that do. For the increasing number of institutions that offer one or more of these products, this book can provide sales staff and management with practical techniques to present these investment services to customers. Annuities, mutual funds and life insurance are "need to know" subjects for many savings institution persons. We hope this book is a pleasant introduction to these products.

Dale Bottom
President
The Institute of Financial Education
July 1988

CREDITS

Instructional Design Department

Veronica Micklin
Project Manager

William Sheldon, C.L.U.
Writer

Ruby Dau-Schmidt
Word Processing Operator

Beverly Johnson
Word Processing Operator

Catherine Scholl
Word Processing Operator

Gaye Matravas
Word Processing Operator

Design and Production Department

Claudia Lamm Wood
Project Coordinator, Editor

Paula Cafferata
Designer

Michael Tapia
Production Manager

This textbook was developed under the direction of Gail Rafter Meneley, Vice President of Marketing, and John Schmidt, AIA, Vice President of Operations.

Institute textbooks are created under the guidance of two department directors: Naomi W. Peralta, Instructional Design, and Robert W. Brown, Design and Production.

The Institute thanks the following individuals who provided assistance and reviewed portions of the manuscript:

Harold Bell, Bank Earnings International

Alan H. Blank, PAMCO Securities and Insurance Services

Donald Maag, United States League of Savings Institutions

Fred Newcomb, Newcomb and Associates

Steve Powell, Kemper Investors Life Insurance Company

Pat Ryan, United Savings of America

In addition, the Institute appreciates the cooperation of:

Richard Alford, American Money Management Group, Inc.

Robert Ewald, Illinois Life and Health Guaranty Association

Richard M. Schlefer, College Retirement Equities Fund

Kay Shepherd, Horizon Federal Savings Bank

Joseph Tillotson, United Savings of America

Sharon Urry, St. Paul Federal Bank for Savings

We gratefully acknowledge the use of material from U.S. League Investment Services, excerpted in Figures 2-2 and 2-3.

Annuities, Mutual Funds & Life Insurance

1

CHAPTER ONE

THE NEED FOR NEW INVESTMENT PRODUCTS

- Definitions of saving, liquidity, risk and return

- Prevailing attitudes toward personal financial planning

- Factors that lead investors to diversify

- Reasons that savings institutions offer nontraditional investment products

Life used to be simple."

Although a cliché this statement is true for the financial services business. A large number of Americans used to depend on deposit accounts and checking accounts as their main savings vehicles. Their only other financial investment was life insurance, which they usually purchased for the death benefit it offered.

Today one of the key words for consumers' financial practices is *diversification*. In their efforts to control risk and provide for long-term financial needs, Americans now use more investment products than ever before. Among the most popular products are mutual funds, annuities and single-premium life insurance. Together these are considered nontraditional products because they represent a departure from the conventional, deposit-type investment services that savings institutions offer.

This chapter presents the major factors that savers must consider. It also examines some recent factors that have led savers to diversify their investment portfolios beyond the traditional savings products and explores why many savings institutions have responded to consumers' needs by offering savers a wider range of investment options.

CONSUMERS' SAVING AND INVESTING BEHAVIOR

Saving means refraining from consumption. When individuals save, they abstain from using part of their money for current purchases in order to have that money in the future. Once people begin saving, they must decide what they will do with those funds.

Two major alternatives are available to the saver. One is to hold the savings in cash form, perhaps in a secret place for safekeeping. Money stored this way offers its owner maximum liquidity, since it is readily available. It does not, however, offer the owner any earnings. Furthermore, the money is susceptible to certain risks, most notably theft. The other alternative is to invest the saved money. Three factors that savers consider when making investment decisions are liquidity, risk and return.

Liquidity

Liquidity refers to an individual's ability to convert an investment into cash at a given time with no significant loss. If an individual can withdraw dollars from an investment at any time without incurring significant loss or cost, that investment is considered very liquid. In contrast, if the individual must incur expenses (such as those involved in the sale of real estate), pay penalties in order to withdraw money, or pay substantial taxes, the investment is considered less liquid.

Risk

Risk is the chance of sustaining loss. The major financial risks that savers face today are summarized below:

- Interest rate risk: uncertainty about the level of interest rates. Both upward and downward changes can affect an investment's relative value.
- Purchasing power risk: possibility that dollars will be less valuable in the future. Inflation

and changes in the value of foreign currencies are among the factors that change the dollar's buying power.

- Tax risk: chance that current regulations specifying the tax treatment of investments and investment income will change and have a negative impact on an investment's value.

While financial risks have always existed, various recent trends and events, described later in the chapter, have made savers' dollars more vulnerable to changes in value. Some savers have responded to these risks by diversifying their assets. (Some of the financial products that many individuals use in their efforts to manage risk are examined in the following chapters.)

Return

Return refers to the profit that one earns by investing. While there are no universal truisms regarding finances and investing, one commonly accepted principle is that return is inversely correlated with risk—that is, investments that offer potentially higher returns generally are riskier than those offering lower yields.

Some investments guarantee an established rate of return; others offer no guarantees. In the past, many savers were attracted to investment products that promised guaranteed interest rates, such as passbook accounts offered by savings institutions. However, as today's investors diversify their investments to manage risk, they also demonstrate a greater willingness to invest their money in certain products that do not guarantee a specific rate of return but have potential for a greater return.

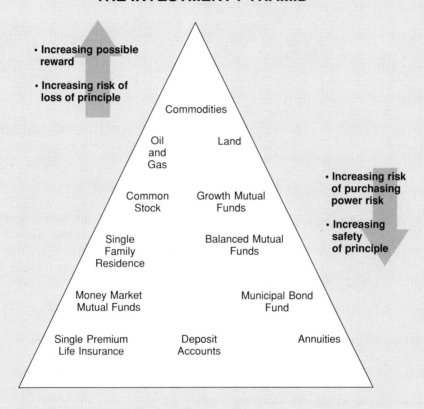

THE INVESTMENT PYRAMID

- **Increasing possible reward**
- **Increasing risk of loss of principle**

- **Increasing risk of purchasing power risk**
- **Increasing safety of principle**

Commodities

Oil and Gas   Land

Common Stock   Growth Mutual Funds

Single Family Residence   Balanced Mutual Funds

Money Market Mutual Funds   Municipal Bond Fund

Single Premium Life Insurance   Deposit Accounts   Annuities

The investment pyramid is a tool that many investors use when they are diversifying their investments. It provides a visual representation of the relationship between risk and return. Investments made at the base of the pyramid entail the least risk to the investor's principle. They do. however, present the highest degree of purchasing power risk. At higher levels of the pyramid an investor is at greater risk of losing principle. At the same time, investments at higher levels of the pyramid offer the investor the potential for higher rates of return.

Many investors use the investment pyramid to structure their investments. One conservative approach to investing calls for people to place the majority of their funds in investments at the bottom of the pyramid. With this approach, dollars are placed in higher-level investments only after the investor has a solid foundation of investments that offer security to principal. Other investors prefer to spread their assets across the levels of the pyramid so that they are not overexposed to purchasing power risk.

PERSONAL INVESTMENT DECISION MAKING TODAY

In 1987, the International Association for Financial Planning conducted a major study to determine the American public's financial attitudes, goals and investments. The results suggested that most Americans were confident about their current financial well-being. At the same time, however, most survey respondents indicated that they were disappointed with their personal net worth.[1]

The survey revealed a strong sense of pessimism regarding personal finances among Americans. By a four-to-three margin, survey respondents indicated a belief that future generations were going to be worse off than they were. While it is impossible to predict how this attitude will affect the financial decision making of current and future generations, this survey does suggest that there will be increased demand for investment products that will allow investors to preserve their financial well-being during difficult times.

The survey also indicated that many Americans find managing their finances and making investment decisions more difficult than in the past. Other studies support this conclusion and also reveal that many individuals seek help with their investment decision making. A 1987 report by the Consumer Federation of America estimated that "there are at least 250,000 and possibly as many as 400,000 individuals nationally who list themselves as financial planners."[2] This statistic supports the belief that a large number of Americans see personal financial planning as a complex, difficult task.

The causes that have contributed to these attitudes are complex. Diverse economic and social trends—at times contradictory factors—have led many savers to respond by diversifying their port-folios by adding nontraditional products.

Experiences with Inflation

One factor that has influenced many consumers' attitudes toward their finances is their experiences with inflation. *Inflation* is a widespread rise in prices that lessens the buying power of each dollar. Inflation cannot be accurately predicted; it is impossible to project the precise percentage by which prices will rise in any period. It is possible, however, to measure inflation that has already occurred.

Inflation and the Consumer Price Index

One common measure of inflation, which the government reports, is the *consumer price index (CPI)*. The CPI measures the changes in price of a *basket*, or group, of goods and services that a typical American consumer might buy. The CPI is expressed in percentage terms to facilitate yearly comparisons and uses 1967 as the base year. Hence, the cost of buying the basket of goods and services in 1967 equals 100% and the cost in other years is expressed as a percentage of the 1967 cost. Figure 1-1 presents the CPI for 1967 to 1987. It also shows the percentage increase that occurred from year to year.

As these graphs illustrate, double-digit inflation troubled Americans for the past 20 years. For example, the cost of living rose by more than 10% during several of these years. Overall, prices of goods and services as measured by the CPI have more than tripled since 1967. In 1987, for example, an individual would have had to pay over $300 to purchase the same goods and services

FIGURE 1-1
Changes in the Consumer Price Index,
1967-1987

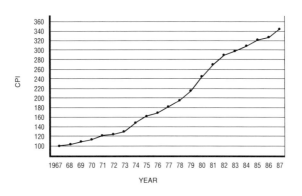

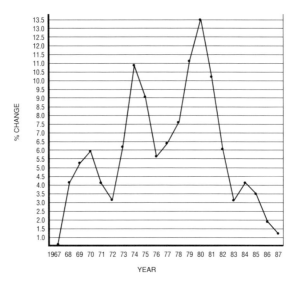

Source: Economic Report of the President (Washington, D.C.:
Government Printing Office, 1987), p. 307.

that cost only $100 in 1967. The cost of housing
has risen more rapidly than the cost of other goods.
In 1987, an individual would have had to spend
$360.20 for every $100 spent on housing in 1967.

Inflation and Savings

Inflation devalues the dollars that individuals have
saved. When prices rise, each dollar has less buying power. Consider an individual that saved
$1,000 in 1975. While saving $1,000 over one
year may not seem like a major effort to many
people today, it was in 1975. During that year,
the average annual wage in the United States was
$10,890.

Suppose that in 1975 this individual deposited $1,000 in a savings account and left that sum,
including earned interest, on deposit until 1987.
Assuming a 7% compound interest rate for the
12 years, the account would have grown to $2,252
in 1987. However, between 1975 and 1987, the
cost of living increased by 114.4%. This means
that the saver's dollars had less buying power in
1987. In 1987, the individual would have needed
$2,144 to have the same real value that $1,000
held in 1975. Therefore, by subtracting $2,144
from $2,252, we see that the actual earning on
the original $1,000, adjusted for inflation, would
be $108.

Concern over the effects of inflation has
caused some savers to seek investments that keep
pace with the inflation rate. However, no investment products can guarantee that savers will retain their buying power when the cost of living
increases. Nevertheless, certain types of investments are often considered good hedges during
times of inflation. Two of these are real estate and
the stock market.

Historically, real estate has proven a good investment during times of inflation. However, most people have limited their real estate investments to the purchase of a home. Few have had the financial resources or the willingness to participate in other real estate investments. Those who did sometimes accomplished this by participating in limited partnerships and other real estate ventures. While these investments once offered many advantages, changes in the tax laws have eliminated some of them. (These changes will be discussed in a later section.)

The stock market sometimes attracts individuals who want to at least retain purchasing power and perhaps even profit during inflationary times. During the past 20 years, some stocks have performed exceptionally well and their value has risen more rapidly than the cost of living. However, other stocks have failed to keep pace with inflation.

One way to evaluate stocks' performance during inflationary times is to compare the change in their values to changes in the cost of living. Figure 1-2 does that by comparing recent changes in the CPI with changes in the Standard and Poor's 500 Index. Standard and Poor's Index measures the general market values of stocks of 500 of the nation's largest corporations. It is accepted as an indicator of the general value of corporate stocks because it represents 70% of the dollar value of the top 5,000 American corporations whose stock is held and traced publicly. As the figure indicates, the consumer price index has risen at a far faster rate than the Standard and Poor's Index. Therefore, an investor would not have kept pace with the inflation rate by investing in stocks that performed as well as the average stock listed with Standard and Poor's. While investors may be at-

FIGURE 1-2
Changes in Living Costs and Stock Prices,
1970-1987

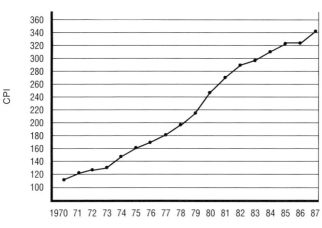

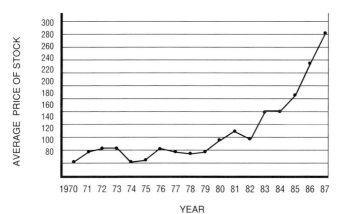

Source: Data for 1970-1986 from Federal Reserve Bulletin,
various issues. The 1987 figure was calculated by the
author. Standard and Poor's Index of 500 Stocks.

tracted by the great profits often associated with stock ownership, many recognize the difficulty of maintaining their assets' values during periods of inflation.

Furthermore, while a stock investment may protect an individual investor from purchasing power risk, it increases exposure to other risks. Investing in the stock market is risky. Stockholders are not guaranteed a specific rate of return. Their profits depend on the performances of the companies in which they invest—in fact, stockholders may lose their principal investment if the companies perform poorly.

Concern over Retirement Security

According to the survey conducted by the International Association for Financial Planning, Americans worry more about retirement than about any other long-term financial goal.[3] Other studies have supported this finding. When *Working Woman* magazine surveyed its readers' financial concerns in 1985, half of the respondents reported that they were worried about being unable to support themselves when they grew old, even though many of them earned higher-than-average salaries.[4]

Why are so many Americans concerned over their financial futures? Some of the most important reasons are:

- inflation
- increased life expectancy
- changes in living patterns.

Inflation
Many people today fear that inflation will continue and the purchasing power of their savings will decrease in the future. Since inflation is un-

predictable, it is impossible to project how much money an individual will require in order to live comfortably during retirement.

Increased Life Expectancy

Americans today have longer life expectancies than ever before. Americans born in 1920—some of whom are the retirees of the 1980s—had an average life expectancy at birth of only 54.1 years.[5] In contrast, for Americans born in 1960 the average life expectancy is 69.7 years, and those born in 1970 are expected to live an average of 70.8 years.

The trend toward longer life expectancies continues. Americans born during 1985 have an average life expectancy of 74.7 years.[6] Therefore, if Americans continue to retire at approximately age 65, they will have more retirement years to enjoy—and in which to support themselves.

Changes in Living Patterns

Changes in living patterns also create concern over one's ability to maintain financial independence during retirement. In the past, many Americans lived in extended families, in which the elderly lived in the same homes with younger family members. The current trend is away from the extended family. Today an increasing number of older persons live alone rather than in family settings. In 1950, 14.4% of all noninstitutionalized persons age 65 and older lived alone. In 1985, this figure was close to 30%.[7] Today over 7.1 million Americans in this age group live alone, and population experts predict that the number will continue to increase in the future.

Many other older Americans head households that they share with their spouses or with other relatives or nonrelatives. Heading one's own household is expensive. Figure 1-3 compares the average annual expenditures of households headed by older people with those of all American households. As the figure indicates, older Americans spend nearly as much as or even more than average households in several categories; yet the size of these households remains smaller than average.

Another expense that some individuals anticipate during their retirement is the cost of living in a nursing home. In 1985, about 1.3 million Americans age 65 or over (around 5%) lived in nursing homes, but this number is expected to climb in coming years.[8] Furthermore, nursing home facilities are expensive, and neither Medicare (the federal insurance program for people 65 and older) nor most private health insurance policies cover nursing care expenses.

In sum, the anticipated costs of retirement have led many individuals to make long-term investment planning a top priority.

Changes in Income Tax Laws

Recent changes in the federal income tax laws have also affected many individuals' investment attitudes and practices. In 1986, Congress overhauled the Internal Revenue Code and made extensive changes in the rules under which Americans calculate the amount of tax they must pay the federal government on their annual incomes. Two specific areas in which the Tax Reform Act of 1986 has affected many investors are tax shelters and tax-sheltered individual retirement accounts.

FIGURE 1-3
Average Annual Expenditures of Households, 1984

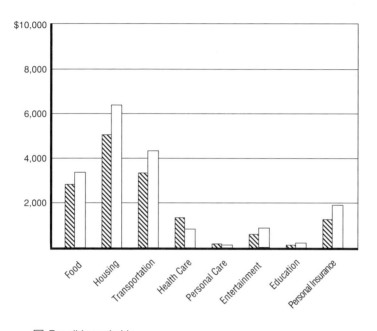

☐ For all households
▨ For all households headed by older Americans*

TOTAL EXPENDITURE**
☐ $20,862
▨ 17,144

NUMBER OF PEOPLE IN HOUSEHOLD
☐ 2.6
▨ 2.1

*Age 65 and above
**Subcategories may not add up to total because some are omitted.

Source: *Statistical Abstract of the United States*, 1987.

Tax Shelters

A *tax shelter* is an investment that provides a legal means of reducing, deferring or escaping taxation. One former type of tax shelter was the real estate limited partnership. This arrangement enabled investors to enjoy many of the tax benefits of owning real estate while avoiding much of the work associated with it. However, the Tax Reform Act of 1986 made major changes in the rules governing real estate partnerships and similar investments that gave investors the tax advantages of incurring business losses for ventures in which they were not actively engaged. As a result, many individuals who might have put their money in these investments are turning to other alternatives.

Tax-Sheltered Retirement Accounts

The Tax Reform Act of 1986 placed restrictions on two popular programs for accumulating retirement funds. First, individual retirement accounts (IRAs) became less beneficial for some individuals. In the past, most taxpayers with earned income could contribute up to $2,000 annually to an IRA and defer paying taxes on that money until they began withdrawing funds, generally during retirement. Under the new tax rules, however, funds placed in IRAs are no longer tax deductible for all taxpayers. Second, the new tax law reduced the contributions that individuals can make to 401(k) plans—savings programs that some employers offer as an employee benefit—to $7,000 annually. These changes have caused many investors to seek other ways to defer taxes and accumulate money for their retirement years.

While the Tax Reform Act of 1986 removed the tax advantages of certain investments, it also enhanced those offered by certain other instruments. Three investments that currently are attracting some investors' dollars are mutual funds based on tax-free government securities, tax-deferred annuities and single-premium whole life insurance. (Each of these tax-advantaged products are described in later chapters.)

Loss of Confidence in the Stock Market

On Monday, October 19, 1987 the prices of stocks sold on American exchanges dropped $500 million. The Dow Jones Industrial Average dropped 22.6%, nearly twice the amount it had dropped on October 28, 1929—the day commonly considered the beginning of the Great Depression.

October 19, 1987 quickly became known as Black Monday. All of the effects of the crash are not yet known. What is certain, however, is that Black Monday destroyed many investors' confidence in the stock market. More specifically, the crash reminded many people how risky investments in stocks and other securities are and that along with their potential for large profits comes a possibility of complete loss. This recognition has led many investors to put at least a portion of their savings into safer investments.

SAVINGS INSTITUTIONS AND NEW PRODUCTS

Each of the above factors has contributed to the present investment environment, in which diversification is a top priority. People have begun to invest in new types of products to reduce their exposure to risk and help them prepare for long-term financial goals. Savings institutions have responded by adding new instruments to their product lines.

When the 1980s opened, savings institutions, rigidly regulated by the Federal Home Loan Bank Board, were limited to offering their customers a small number of traditional savings products. In 1980, a major change in the savings business occurred as the Depository Institutions Deregulation Committee was empowered to phase out most savings account regulations. Once regulations were loosened, savings institutions moved quickly to offer their customers a broader line of products. By June 1987, about 25% of all savings institutions offered mutual funds. According to an industry survey, close to 50% planned to offer mutual funds by the end of 1988. The move to offer other nontraditional products has been equally strong.

The addition of mutual funds, annuities and other nontraditional products has been a major change for savings institutions. Many institutions were accustomed to offering deposit and loan products that they themselves designed, priced and delivered. In contrast, the nontraditional products that their customers now demand are originated elsewhere. Also, when savings institutions sell nontraditional products, they are in effect sharing their customers with other businesses, serving as the conduit between the customer and a mutual fund or insurance company.

Strengthening Relationships with Customers

A savings institution's most valuable assets are its relationships with its customers. No institution can survive without customers to serve. However, the reverse is not true. Customers do not have to depend on any one financial institution to satisfy their needs. Hundreds of other financial service providers—including other savings institutions—offer consumers savings, investment and lending services. Each of these service providers represents competition for a savings institution.

One goal of a savings institution is to retain—and, if possible, increase—its share of customers. While each institution devises its own strategy for meeting this goal, certain common strategies are evident. One currently popular strategy is to diversify the institution's product line to offer the products that customers demand. Two major arguments generally used in support of this strategy are consumers' preference for full-service providers and the need to keep customers from taking their business elsewhere.

The One-Stop Shopping Concept

One of the arguments presented by advocates of product diversification is that consumers prefer to use one provider for meeting most of their financial service needs. The trend of consumers to diversify their investments supports this argument. Recent surveys indicate that many people are attracted to financial institutions that offer the diversification they desire under one roof.

Figure 1-4 shows how respondents in one major survey of savers identified the factor most important to them in deciding to maintain accounts in their savings institutions. Variety of financial services was named more important than an institution's business hours, service charges, thoroughness of service, loan rates and several other factors.

A recent survey undertaken by *American Banker* also supported the popularity of full-service providers. According to the newspaper's 1987

FIGURE 1-4
Factors Important to Consumers in Choosing a Savings Institution

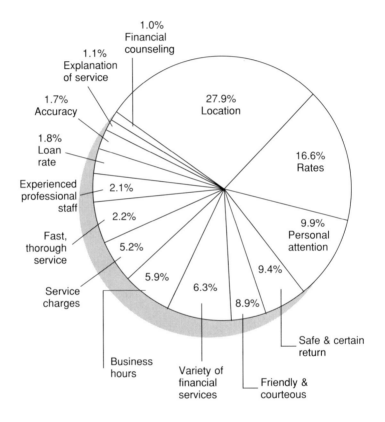

Source: *1986 Saver's Survey* (Chicago: U.S. League of Savings Institutions, 1987).

fourth annual survey of consumer attitudes, over one-third of all consumers prefer doing all of their financial business with one provider. Many of those individuals said they would prefer to purchase mutual funds and insurance products from the institutions at which they bank.[9]

Consumers' desire to do most of their financial business with one institution complements a theory long popular in the financial services business, namely, that the strength of the relationship between a customer and a financial institution is directly related to the number of services the customer uses at that institution. In this theory, a customer who has a deposit account, a credit card and direct deposit service with an institution has a stronger relationship with that institution than a customer who uses only one of its services. Therefore, by offering customers more options, savings institutions create opportunities for enhancing their customer relationships.

Preventing Outflow to Competitors

The second argument used by many diversification advocates is closely related to the first. Because of the current emphasis on personal financial planning in newspapers, television and other media, consumers are more knowledgeable about their needs and available products. Advocates of product diversification believe that if an institution fails to provide customers with products they want, they will go to another provider to obtain them—and when that happens, they are likely to transfer *all* of their accounts to that provider. As a result, the original institution will lose a valuable asset—its relationships with its customers— if it fails to provide the products they want.

Generating Fee Income

A second reason that savings institutions offer their customers new types of investment services is the opportunity to earn revenue through fees. Fee income has become increasingly important to savings institutions' financial health.

In the past, savings institutions depended almost exclusively on spread as a source of income. *Spread* is the difference between the return on investments (loans) and the cost of funds (deposits). When interest rates were relatively stable, savings institutions could set their savings and lending rates at levels that provided a consistent spread. In recent years, however, interest rates have been more volatile, making spread income less dependable as a source of income. To generate income under these new conditions, institutions have begun to depend more heavily on fees as a source of revenue. Adding new investment services is one way to earn fee income. When savings institutions offer mutual funds or insurance products, they earn fees from the transactions their customers make.

FOOTNOTES

[1]"Americans Cope with Their Finances" (Public opinion survey conducted by the International Association for Financial Planning, June 2, 1987, Atlanta, Georgia).

[2]Barbara Roper, *Financial Planning Abuses: A Growing Problem* (Washington, DC: Consumer Federation of America, 1987), p. 11.

[3]"Americans Cope with Their Finances."

[4]"Readers Survey," *Working Woman*, Nov. 1985, p. 76.

[5]*Statistical Abstract of the United States: 1987*, 107th ed. (Washington, DC: U.S. Department of Commerce) Table 105, p. 69.

[6]*Statistical Abstract.*

[7]American Association of Retired Persons and Administration on Aging, *A Profile of Older Americans, 1986* (Washington, DC: U.S. Department of Health and Human Services, 1987), p. 3.

[8]*Profile of Older Americans.*

[9]"One-Stop Shopping Lures Middle Market," *American Banker*, Sept. 28, 1987, pp. 1, 46.

2

CHAPTER TWO

MUTUAL FUNDS

- Definition of a mutual fund

- Mutual fund classifications

- Steps involved in the purchase of shares in a mutual fund

- Investor considerations in purchasing a mutual fund

O VER THE LAST 10 YEARS, mutual funds have become an extremely popular method of investing by the American public. According to the Investment Company Institute, assets of the mutual fund industry totaled $800 billion in 1987. Furthermore, research surveys show that a large number of consumers who have never invested in mutual funds are thinking of doing so in the future.[1]

Why have mutual funds attracted so many dollars? Two reasons stand out. First, mutual funds allow investors to own corporate stocks and bonds or government securities without incurring all of the risks and costs involved in buying and trading these securities individually. Second, mutual funds are now offered by commercial banks and savings institutions. Thus, some people who would not invest in mutual funds through brokerage houses are willing to do so when they are offered by savings institutions or banks because they are familiar with and trust these institutions.[2]

DEFINITION OF A MUTUAL FUND

A *mutual fund* is a company that makes investments on behalf of its owners. The owners of the mutual fund are the people and institutions that have purchased shares in it.[3] The mutual fund then uses its shareholders' combined funds to purchase and manage a portfolio of stocks, bonds and other investments. The portfolio remains in existence on a continuing basis, although the individual securities that comprise it may differ each day.

REGULATION OF MUTUAL FUNDS

Mutual funds are regulated at the federal level by the Securities and Exchange Commission (SEC). The SEC uses four major federal statutes in its regulation of mutual funds.

The first law is the Securities Act of 1933, which, among other requirements, specifies the information that every mutual fund must file with the SEC. The 1933 act also designates the information that a mutual fund must provide for potential investors before they purchase shares and limits the types of advertisements that a mutual fund may use.

The second major law is the Securities Exchange Act of 1934, which governs the purchase and sale of mutual fund shares. This law gives particular attention to preventing fraud. The third law is the Investment Advisers Act of 1940, which regulates the activities of investment advisors for mutual funds. The fourth law is the Investment Company Act of 1940. This act, which has been amended many times since its passage, contains extensive details on the operation of mutual funds. Included are rules concerning the fees and charges a fund may impose on its shareholders. The law also specifies how a fund must invest its holdings in order to avoid conflicts of interest. In addition to these federal laws, mutual funds are subject to the laws of the states in which they operate.

MANAGEMENT OF MUTUAL FUNDS

Participation in a mutual fund provides shareholders with professional management of investment dollars that would be unavailable to them if they acted on their own. Since the business of a mutual fund is the investment of money, its managers are primarily financial advisors and analysts with the responsibility for making investment decisions. These investment specialists research market conditions, inflation, interest rate trends and other economic factors. They also study general business publications, corporate and government financial reports and surveys and other research instruments in order to determine how well securities in the fund's portfolios are performing. Such securities are bought and sold based on these experts' analyses and recommendations.

MUTUAL FUND CLASSIFICATIONS

Not all mutual funds are alike. One way they differ is in their investment objectives. Individual mutual funds vary in their investment goals because they are aimed at serving distinct segments of the investment market (see Chapter 1). For example, the goal of some mutual funds is to generate a regular flow of current income. A fund with this objective may attract retired individuals who want to receive a regular income from their investments. In contrast, some other mutual funds seek long-term capital growth and forgo current income. These funds are favored by investors who want to accumulate money for a future expense, such as the purchase of a second home. Still other mutual funds aim at providing income tax advantages for their shareholders. Finally, some funds seek to provide investors with a relatively safe way to invest funds on a short-term basis. Thus, one way investors choose among mutual funds is by learning the funds' investment objectives and comparing them to their own.

The managers of a mutual fund focus on the fund's objective in making their investment decisions. For example, the managers of a fund that emphasizes capital appreciation may invest in new industries, newly formed corporations or other ventures that they predict will grow in value. In contrast, the managers of a mutual fund aimed at generating current income may invest in companies that regularly pay high dividends.

The number of identifiable categories of mutual funds has increased along with the number of individual mutual fund companies. In 1975 most mutual funds could be classified into seven categories. Today, the Investment Company Institute, the national association of investment companies, classifies mutual funds into 22 broad categories according to their basic investment objectives. The most common categories of funds are presented below.

Aggressive Growth Funds

Growth funds seek maximum capital gains with little concentration on regular flow of income. Growth funds generally invest in the common stocks of companies that demonstrate potential for growth. Some growth funds invest in businesses that may not be attractive to conservative investors, such as new industries, companies that have suffered from an economic downturn or industries that are not currently popular among investors.

Income Funds

Income funds seek a high level of current income. One group of income funds limits their investments to debt investments (bonds) while the other

FAMILY OF FUNDS

Many mutual fund investment companies offer what they term a "family of funds." These are a diversified group of mutual funds with investment objectives to suit a wide variety of financial goals.

One such hypothetical group would be as follows:

Income Funds	Growth Funds

GOVERNMENT SECURITIES FUND
U.S. government securities for preservation of capital along with current income.

CORPORATE BOND FUND
High-grade bonds for current income with preservation of capital.

TOTAL RETURN FUND
Stocks and bonds for above average current income; potential for growth of both capital and income.

MONEY MARKET FUND
Money market instruments geared for capital preservation, liquidity, and current income.

GROWTH STOCK FUND
Common stocks for long-term growth of capital and future income rather than current yield.

DEVELOPMENT FUND
Primarily stocks of newer companies for long-term growth of capital with a moderate amount of current income.

QUALITY STOCK FUND
High-quality common stocks yielding current income and presenting potential for long-term growth of both capital and income.

The idea behind the family of funds concept is to provide the customer with a single source of varied types of fund investments. According to fluctuating economic conditions or varying customer preferences, the shareowner may make frequent changes in investment portfolios. Once the initial sales fees are paid, switches in fund investments are usually allowed without additional sales loads.

type invests in equities (stocks). Income bond funds generally invest in a mix of corporate and government bonds. Income equity funds invest primarily in stocks from companies with good histories of paying dividends.

Balanced Funds

These mutual funds seek to earn both capital gains and current income. Balanced funds generally invest in high-grade common stocks, bonds, preferred stocks and other fixed-income securities. Balanced funds offer fewer capital gains than growth funds and smaller yields than income funds, but they are usually less risky than growth funds.

Ginnie Mae Funds

These mutual funds invest in mortgage-backed securities investments issued by the Government National Mortgage Association, known as GNMA or Ginnie Mae. Mutual funds included in this category invest the majority of their portfolios in mortgage-backed securities.

Long-Term Municipal Bond Funds

These companies invest in bonds issued by states and municipalities to finance public projects such as the construction of schools, highways, airports or sports stadiums. In most cases, income earned on these securities is not taxed by the federal government, but it may be taxed by state and local authorities.

Money Market Mutual Funds

Money market mutual funds offer investors high liquidity and low risk. These popular mutual funds invest in short-term securities such as U.S. Treasury bills, jumbo bank certificates of deposit and commercial paper (short-term IOUs issued by large corporations).

U.S. Government Securities

These low-risk mutual funds invest in a variety of government securities including U.S. Treasury bills, notes, bonds and obligations of U.S. government agencies.

PURCHASING A MUTUAL FUND

Investors can purchase shares in a mutual fund either directly from the fund or through individuals such as financial planners and counselors, savings institution employees, insurance agents and stockbrokers. Most funds require a minimum amount of money for an initial investment. For example, a fund may require an individual to purchase at least $500 in shares in order to become an owner. Some funds also specify minimum amounts for subsequent investments. For instance, a fund may require that the investor purchase at least $50 worth of shares each time he or she wishes to make an additional investment in the fund.

Investors can learn about mutual funds from several sources of information, as shown in Figure 2-1. Many individuals do their own research or rely on information received from counselors at their savings institutions or banks when deciding how to invest their money. According to another survey, fewer than one in five investors have a broker, accountant, financial planner or lawyer

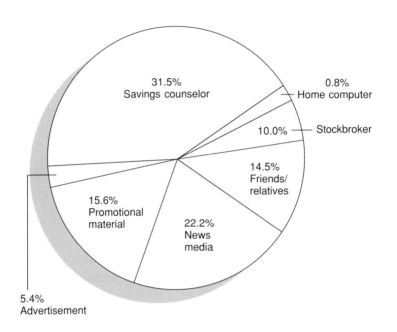

FIGURE 2-1
Most Important Sources of Financial Information

31.5%
Savings counselor

0.8%
Home computer

10.0% —— Stockbroker

14.5%
Friends/
relatives

15.6%
Promotional
material

22.2%
News
media

5.4%
Advertisement

Source: 1986 *Saver's Survey* (Chicago: U.S. League of Savings Institutions, 1987).

who is familiar with their finances.[4] Since 78% of the individuals who responded to this poll invested money in mutual funds, many people who purchase mutual funds do so without hiring someone to manage their individual investment portfolios.

Counselors in Savings Institutions

The tendency of many people to make investment decisions with information received from savings counselors at their savings institution is supported by the data in Figure 2-1. According to the survey on which the figure is based, 31.5% of the respondents considered their savings counselors as their main source of investment information. In contrast, only 10% of persons polled cited stockbrokers as their most important information source.

News Media

A second important source of information for prospective mutual fund investors is the news media. The most commonly used types of print media are newspapers and magazines.

Many newspapers report on mutual funds in their business or financial pages. Newspapers often present daily price reports and articles that describe and recommend various mutual funds. An explanation of how to use newspaper tables to determine the price of a mutual fund is given later in this chapter.

Two types of magazines provide information about mutual funds: those for investors in general and those developed for particular segments of the investor population. *Money, Fortune* and *Changing Times* magazines are examples of the first category, while *Working Woman* and *Modern Maturity* (the latter published by the American Association of Retired Persons) are among those in the second.

Subscription Services

Another popular source of investment information is subscription investment advisory services. These services generally publish investment guides and newsletters filled with information about investment opportunities. These publications provide background information on mutual funds and other investments. Subscription services differ from magazines in that they make buy and sell recommendations. They generally are not affiliated with brokerage firms or other investment sellers and therefore do not profit from the transactions their readers make. For this reason, many investors believe they are valuable sources of objective information. Two well-known investment advisories are the *Value Line Investment Survey* and *Standard and Poor's Outlook*. These and other investment advisory publications are usually available at public libraries.

Prospectuses and Reports

Mutual funds also publish documents that can be useful for investors. The most common types are prospectuses and reports. A *prospectus* is a written description of the fund's investment objectives, policies and performance. It also provides information on the fund's management and investment advisors. Figure 2-2 presents an excerpt from the prospectus of one mutual fund. This portion shows the type of investments that will be in the fund's portfolio and how the fund's managers expect to use them to meet the fund's objectives.

A potential investor can also use a prospectus to learn about services that the fund offers its shareholders. Among services that may be described in a prospectus are check-writing privi-

FIGURE 2-2
Excerpt from Prospectus

ADVANCE AMERICA CORPORATE BOND FUND

The investment objective of this Fund is to earn a high level of current income consistent with investment in short-, intermediate- and long-term securities. The Fund invests, under normal market conditions, at least 65% of the value of its total assets in bonds paying current income issued by corporations. Its remaining investments will consist of investments eligible for the Advance America U.S. Government Securities and GNMA Mortgage Securities Funds; obligations of international agencies such as the International Bank for Reconstruction and Development, the Inter-American Development Bank and the Asian Development Bank; and money market instruments such as commercial paper, bankers' acceptances and certificates of deposit. The Fund follows the policy that all of its debt investments will consist of those investments considered to be of "investment grade" quality, or equivalent.

Corporate bonds are generally considered to be investment grade of they are rated in one of the four highest investment ratings categories by any of the nationally recognized rating agencies, including either Moody's Investors Service, Inc. ("Moody's") or Standard & Poor's Corporation ("Standard & Poor's"). Unrated securities may be purchased if, in the opinion of the investment adviser, the securities are of a similar quality to those rated within these four rating categories. Bonds rated in the fourth investment grading category, while still investment grade, are not considered high-grade and generally involve greater volatility of price and risk of principal and income than bonds in the three highest categories. Higher quality, shorter-term income producing debt securities may not earn as high a level of current income as lower quality, longer-term securities which, however, are subject to more market and credit risk and have greater pricer fluctuations.

Source: U.S. League of Savings Institutions, 1988.

leges or automatic withdrawals for individuals who wish to receive regular income from their investments. The prospectus may also explain how dividends earned by the fund's investments will be distributed to investors. Some funds offer dividend reinvestment plans, in which the investor's earnings from the fund are automatically used to purchase additional shares. This service may be of particular interest to investors who wish to increase their holdings in a fund.

The second type of document, the *annual* or *semiannual report*, contains the fund's financial statements and lists all the securities in the fund's portfolio. Figure 2-3 presents a sample of the financial information contained in a typical report.

These reports also summarize business and economic developments that affected the portfolio's value over the year. For example, if the fund made a large profit because it invested in oil company stocks at a time when the price of oil surged, it may include this information in the report. Similarly, if the fund lost money during a period of general price decline in the stock market, it may report this factor.

Both prospectuses and reports are easy for potential investors to obtain—in fact, federal regulations require that an individual be presented with a prospectus before he or she makes a decision on buying shares in a mutual fund. However, while investors find prospectuses accessible, they do not always find them easy to read. In some cases, the specialized terminology, technical writing style or small print size in prospectuses make it difficult or impossible for some individuals to read and comprehend the complete document. In these instances clear, verbal explanations of material presented in the prospectuses can help an investor make an informed decision.

INVESTOR CONSIDERATIONS IN THE PURCHASE OF MUTUAL FUNDS

Investments in mutual funds have benefited many individuals. As with all investments, however, investors must consider many factors before de-

FIGURE 2-3
Financial Statement from Annual Report

Asset Management Fund for Savings Institutions, Inc.
Mortgage Securities Performance Portfolio
Statement of Net Assets
October 31, 1987

	Percentage of Net Assets	Par (000)	Value
Mortgage-Related Securities	94.3%		
Federal National Mortgage Association Bonds			
13.20% due 09/12/88		$ 4,000	$ 4,187,500
11.15% due 06/12/95		6,000	6,540,000
			10,727,500
Government National Mortgage Association Obligations			
11.50% due 05/15/10 to 11/15/15		23,542	24,682,072
10.50% due 09/15/15 to 02/15/16		17,575	17,822,198
10.00% due 10/15/09 to 10/15/17		56,029	55,398,233
9.50% due 06/15/09 to 12/15/16		64,271	61,760,423
9.00% due 09/15/04 to 03/15/17		100,645	94,354,545
8.50% due 09/15/16 to 03/15/17		49,803	44,994,283
			299,011,754
Total Mortgage-Related Securities (Cost $322,774,168)			309,739,254
Loans of Federal Funds	4.8%		
6.875% due 11/02/87 (Cost $15,742,000)		15,742	15,742,000
Total Investments in Securities (Cost $338,516,168*) (Note A)	99.1%		325,481,254
Other Assets in Excess of Liabilities	.9%		2,920,575
Net Assets applicable to 31,723,156 shares of Common Stock issued and outstanding	100.0%		$328,401,829
Net Asset Value, offering and redemption price per share ($328,401,829 ÷ 31,723,156)			$ 10.35

* Aggregate cost for Federal income tax purposes. The aggregate gross
unrealized appreciation (depreciation) for all securities is as follows:
excess of value over tax cost $1,857,149; excess of tax cost over value
($14,892,063).

ciding to add mutual funds to a portfolio. Among these concerns are earnings, costs, risks, convenience, income taxes and administration. The following sections examine these considerations from the investor's point of view.

Earnings

Investors may profit from their mutual fund investments in three ways: through dividends; through capital gains earned by the fund and passed on to shareholders; and through capital gains earned upon redemption of shares.

Dividends

Dividends consist of the earnings that the fund is paid from the securities in which it invests. These earnings may include dividends directly paid out by the issuers of the securities or in the form of interest earned on the securities. For example, assume that Mutual Fund A owns stock in Corporation X. Since Corporation X has had a profitable year, its board of directors votes to pay a dividend to its stockholders. As one of these stockholders, Mutual Fund A will receive dividend payments from Corporation X. The share owners in Mutual Fund A will in turn profit from these dividends. Interest paid to a mutual fund benefits shareholders in a similar way. For example, when Mutual Fund B earns interest through its investments in municipal bonds, that money becomes part of the dividends passed along to Mutual Fund B's shareholders. Dividends are paid to mutual fund shareholders on a regular schedule (monthly, quarterly, semiannually or annually) that is stipulated in the fund's prospectus.

Capital Gains

Capital gains refers to money earned when an investment that has increased in value is sold. Mutual fund shareholders may benefit from two types of capital gains.

The first type of capital gains occurs when the mutual fund sells an investment in its portfolio at a higher price than it paid for it. For example, suppose Mutual Fund C purchases 1,000 shares of stock in XYZ Inc. at $64 a share. It sells those shares two years later at $84 a share, realizing $20,000 in capital gains. Mutual Fund C passes this profit along, together with capital gains earned through other transactions, to its shareholders when it issues its annual capital gains distributions.[5]

Shareholders in mutual funds may also earn capital gains when they *redeem* their shares, that is, sell them back to the fund. Shareholders who wish to withdraw their investments from a mutual fund do so by selling their shares back to the fund at the NAV. Since the NAV fluctuates as the value of a mutual fund's investments changes, shareholders can gain by redeeming their shares at a higher price than they paid for them.

Consider a hypothetical shareholder who experiences a capital gain through selling his shares in a mutual fund. Eric Stephen owns 187 shares in Mutual Fund C that he received as a gift from his grandmother 12 years ago. At that time, Mutual Fund C held in its portfolio 10,000 shares of stock in Q Corporation, a new business. Last year, Q Corporation became the federal government's main supplier of small hinges used in curbside mailboxes. The price of Q Corporation stock soared, as did the NAV of Mutual Fund C. When Eric Stephen redeems his shares for a downpayment on a house, he finds that they are worth far more than his grandmother paid for them. The difference between the purchase price and the redemption price of the shares constitutes a capital gain for him.

Costs

The investor should consider two categories of costs associated with the purchase of mutual funds. To invest in a mutual fund, an individual must pay the price of the shares to be purchased and, in some cases, a sales commission. The first consists of minimums on both initial investments and reinvestments established by the fund. Individuals who are accustomed to the deposit rules for deposit accounts may be unwilling or unable to invest in a fund that imposes a high minimum deposit requirement. Thus, it is important that the investor consider how a fund's investment dollar requirements meet his or her intended plans.

Price of Shares

The fund determines the price of a share in a mutual fund at least once each day and sometimes twice daily. To calculate the share price, the fund determines the total value of its investments' dividends and capital gains and adds in a factor for expenses (expenses include the salaries paid to the fund's financial managers and analysts). Then it divides this total by the number of shares outstanding to arrive at the price per share. The price per share in a mutual fund is known as the *net asset value (NAV)*.

Investors are not required to purchase whole shares when they invest in mutual funds, because mutual funds sell fractional as well as full shares. Therefore, one may invest a specific amount of money regardless of the per-share price. For example, if an investor wishes to invest $1,000 in a no-load fund containing shares with an offering price of $16, he or she can purchase 62.5 shares.

Fees

The second cost category an investor must consider is the load, or sales fee, some mutual funds charge. Loads generally range from 2% to 8.5% of the invested amount. When an investor purchases shares in a *load fund*, the load is added to the NAV. The sum of the load and the NAV is referred to as the *offering price* or *buy price*. Shares in *no-load funds* are sold for the NAV. Many funds charge a fee of up to 8.5% when shares are purchased or redeemed. While some load funds may claim that historically their profitability has surpassed the amount that investors pay in fees, the investor cannot be certain that they will continue to perform as well in the future. Therefore, a high load might negate any earnings that the investor realizes. This concern is more critical when mutual funds are being considered as short-term investments. Short-term ownership might allow the investor less time to regain the money that he or she spent on the sales fee. For this reason, some investors are attracted to low-load or no-load mutual funds.

Figure 2-4 illustrates the price information on mutual funds typically reported in the financial pages of newspapers. Fund names are listed in alphabetical order in the first column. When one company manages more than one fund, the funds are referred to as a *family of funds* and are listed under the same heading. The number in the second column is the NAV for that mutual fund at the end of the previous business day. The third column lists the offering price of each share—the

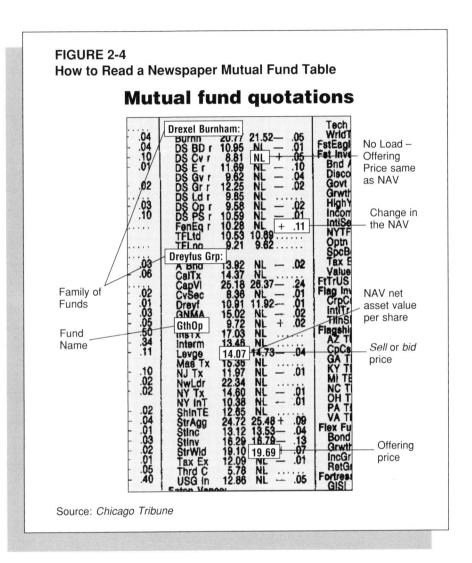

FIGURE 2-4
How to Read a Newspaper Mutual Fund Table

Mutual fund quotations

Source: *Chicago Tribune*

NAV plus the load. If the fund is a no-load fund, the letters *NL* may be listed in this column. The final column shows the net change in the share price since the last quotation. Thus, from this column an investor can learn how the value of a share (the NAV) changed, in cents, during the last trading day.

Some load and no-load mutual funds charge other types of fees. One example is *entry fees*—charges that are imposed when an investor enters the fund for the first time. An entry fee is different from a load because it is not calculated according to the number of shares an individual purchases. Another example is *exit* or *back-end loads*—charges incurred when one leaves the fund. These fees generally are service fees and may or may not be related to sales charges. Some back-end load funds impose a higher fee if the investor redeems the shares within a short period, such as less than a year, and a lower fee if the investor holds the shares for a longer period. In addition, some mutual funds charge owners separate fees if they are holding the shares as part of an IRA or Keogh account.

Risks

Mutual funds entail risks. Neither the rate of return nor the return of the full principal investment amount is guaranteed to the mutual fund investor.

Investors cannot rely on income from all mutual funds with the same certainty that they can for income on certificates of deposit or government bonds. While some funds, such as money market funds, entail little risk others, such as aggressive growth funds, can be very risky. The money that mutual funds return to their shareholders as dividends comes from money the funds earn in interest or dividends. Business and economic conditions and other factors can cause the interest and dividends paid by the investments in a mutual fund's portfolio to increase, decrease or even discontinue. For example, if a mutual fund earns fewer dollars from its investments in one quarter than it did during the previous quarter, its shareholders will see this drop reflected in their dividends. If the mutual fund's investments continue to perform poorly, the shareholders will continue to see their dividend returns diminish. Therefore, shareholders in mutual funds risk losing anticipated income.

When the securities owned by a mutual fund lose value, their per-share value will reflect that loss. This loss in value to the fund's shareholders can occur in one of two ways. First, if the mutual fund trades its securities at a loss, it receives no capital gains to distribute to its shareholders. As a result, the shareholders will not receive the capital gains they may have expected to earn on their investments. Second, if the mutual fund's portfolio contains securities that have decreased in value, shareholders who redeem their shares may receive less money than they originally paid for them.

While mutual funds do involve risks, many investors believe that the professional management that mutual funds offer reduces the risks they as individual investors would otherwise face. Successfully managing an investment portfolio requires extensive knowledge of individual enterprises and industries and of the national and global economies. Time is another requirement, since securities transactions often must be conducted within a short period—perhaps hours or even minutes—in order to achieve the investor's objective. Professional financial managers can be hired to direct an investment portfolio, but these services are expensive and generally are used only by wealthy investors. Mutual funds put the expertise and vigilance of a professional team of investment analysts and managers to work for individuals to whom they would otherwise be inaccessible.

Exposure to risk is a particularly important consideration for investors who are accustomed to depositing their money in federally insured deposit accounts. Such investors may want extensive information on how a mutual fund invests its money in order to ascertain their personal tolerance for risk. In some cases, risk considerations are especially important for older investors who are planning to use their investment dollars for their retirement. If investors must redeem shares in a mutual fund investment during a temporary downturn in the market, they may lose money.[6] However, this concern may be less critical to investors who would be able to hold their shares in anticipation of the fund's recovery.

Convenience

Many investors choose mutual funds because they value the ease with which they can make these investments. Three aspects of mutual funds that many individuals find convenient are liquidity, diversifiability and reinvestment options.

Liquidity

Liquidity refers to the ease with which an investment can be converted into cash. Mutual funds are relatively liquid investments, because by law they must be ready to redeem shares on any day that they are open for business.[7] Under securities regulations, mutual funds are obligated to buy back their own shares at the NAV rate as recalculated at the end of each business day.

Redemption procedures differ among funds. Some funds require that an owner provide them with a written request specifying the number of shares that he or she wishes to redeem. After receiving this notification, the fund sends a check to the investor—generally within a week. Some mutual funds are even more liquid: They allow shareholders to write drafts against their holdings. Money market funds can be redeemed through wire or phone transactions. These highly liquid funds usually can be redeemed within 24 hours.

Another important liquidity protection is offered under the Savings Investor Protection Corporation (SIPC). This government agency insures investors' accounts in brokerage firms for up to $100,000. The investor's original principal investment in stocks or mutual funds is not insured; there can be no guarantee with a fluctuating investment. SIPC insurance protects the current market value of the investor's holdings in case the brokerage house experiences financial difficulties. Investors' funds can not be dissipated in bankruptcy proceedings. Many brokerage firms offer supplementary insurance that increases the amount of insurance up to a total of $500,000.

Diversification

Mutual funds provide an easy way to *diversify* one's portfolio—to own an interest in several different securities. According to the Investment Company Act of 1940, a mutual fund may have no more than 5% of its assets in any one company. As a result, an investor who buys shares in a mutual fund automatically buys into at least 20 different securities. Regulations also forbid a mutual fund to own more than 10% of the outstanding shares of a single company. Thus, participation in a mutual fund offers an investor a portfolio that ensures the safety of principal associated with spreading risk over a large number of investments.

Reinvestment Options

When shareholders in mutual funds earn dividends on their shares, they generally are permitted to reinvest their dividends with the funds automatically. This reinvestment option allows investors to acquire a larger portion of the fund more easily than if they made each purchase separately. With some mutual funds, reinvestment purchases are made without loads even if the funds charge loads for other share purchases. Thus, the shareholders in some mutual funds not only enjoy convenience; they also save money when they reinvest their dividends.

Income Taxes

The income that investors receive on their mutual fund investments is taxed similarly to investments made directly instead of through the mutual fund. Therefore, capital gains that the fund passes along to investors are treated as capital gains income on investors' tax returns. Likewise, if a mutual fund invests in securities that are exempt from federal income taxes, the fund's shareholders receive tax-exempt income. Many investors choose tax-exempt mutual funds for precisely this reason.

Each year, mutual funds send reports to every shareholder reporting how much money that individual made through dividends and redemptions in the fund during the year. The investor must report this income on his or her income tax return. When mutual funds are held in an IRA, Keogh, tax-deferred annuity or other tax-deferred plan, the investor pays taxes on the investment income when he or she withdraws funds from the plan.

Administrative Assistance

Many investors favor mutual funds because of the administrative assistance they offer their shareholders. In particular, record keeping and safeguarding of documents are easier for mutual fund shareholders than they are for owners of stocks, bonds and Treasury bills. Mutual funds collect dividends and interest earned on their investments and take care of other duties that owners of stocks, bonds and government securities must perform themselves.

Mutual funds also make it easy for investors to track the value of their investments. They generally provide their shareholders with quarterly statements reporting investments, withdrawals, dividends and capital gains distributions and reinvestments. Furthermore, at the end of each year, mutual funds send shareholders a statement showing the dividends and capital gains paid to them during the year. This statement helps shareholders when they prepare their income tax returns.

Unlike owners of some other investments, shareholders in mutual funds need not be concerned with the safekeeping of negotiable instruments. Owners of stocks must securely store their certificates or pay someone to do so. Bondholders and owners of Treasury bills must also secure documents that prove their ownership. In contrast, while shareholders in mutual funds may be part owners of many securities, they need not store separate documents to protect their ownership rights in a diversified portfolio. The mutual fund does all of this for them.

FOOTNOTES

[1]*The Unidex Report,* Part 1 (Unidex Corporation, April 1987) and *Bank and Thrift Mutual Funds: An Emerging $40 Billion Market* (Chicago: Market Facts, Inc., 1984).

[2]*Bank and Thrift Mutual Funds,* p. 1.

[3]Institutions that invest money in order to fund future payments are often referred to as *institutional investors.* Examples of institutional investors are pension funds, insurance companies, foundations and endowments.

[4]"The *Money* Readers' Poll," *Money,* Feb. 1987, pp. 194-197.

[5]The distribution of dividends and capital gains to shareholders in mutual funds is regulated by the SEC. According to federal law, mutual funds must distribute to shareholders at least 98% of their taxable income each year. In complying with this regulation, mutual funds qualify as a category of business that does not have to pay taxes on the profits it earns. Since the fund itself is not taxed, the shareholders receive a greater portion of its profits than they would if the fund were responsible for taxes on these earnings. Of course, the shareholders must declare these profits as taxable income.

[6]The net value may also be reduced if the fund's managers sell assets to deliberately incur a capital loss as part of a long-term plan. While the strategy may benefit shareholders who remain in the fund for the long term, it may be a disadvantage to individuals who redeem their shares while the NAV is low.

[7]A closed-end investment company offers a fixed number of shares. Closed-end shares are bought, sold and traded in the open market just as corporate securities are. In contrast, open-end companies (usually known as mutual funds) continuously offer their shares for sale. There is no limit to the number of shares an open-end company may offer. The information in this section refers to open-end mutual funds. Closed-end investment company shares, less common today, are not redeemed by their issuer in this manner.

3

CHAPTER THREE

FIXED ANNUITIES

- Why people invest in annuities
- Basic annuity terminology
- Methods of distribution of annuity funds
- Mathematical base of fixed annuities
- Investor considerations in purchasing fixed annuities

H OW DO YOU THINK most people react to the prospect of an investment that offers them a guaranteed annual income after they retire, no matter how long they live? As you might expect, many are very interested. That is the appeal of annuities.

Annuities are often called "life insurance in reverse." Life insurance creates an estate immediately upon the insured's death, thus replacing some portion of that person's future income. This protection is particularly important when the insured dies prematurely and is survived by individuals who are dependent on his or her anticipated future income. Thus, life insurance can be considered protection against "not living long enough."

An annuity, in contrast, protects against "living too long." While many people agree that a long life is a blessing, they also acknowledge that they do not wish to outlast the savings they have accumulated for retirement. This concern underlies one of the basic attractions of annuities: By assuring continued payments for an unlimited number of years, annuities guarantee that the insured will not deplete his or her source of income.

BASIC TERMINOLOGY

Since annuities are contracts offered by insurance companies, much of the terminology used to describe them comes from the insurance field. In this section, we will define some terms.

An *annuity* is a policy contract that agrees to pay the insured a regular income over a specified period of years. When an individual purchases an annuity policy, he or she agrees to pay the insurance company a certain amount of money in exchange for this income. The time period over which the insurance company promises to provide income varies. The contract may specify an exact number of years or the individual's lifetime—an unspecified number. The term annuity usually refers to the contract made between an individual and an insurance company; it is also used to describe the income that the individual receives under the contract.

The payments one makes for an annuity are referred to as *premiums*. Premiums, like money placed in a deposit account, earn interest, and these amounts increase in value while the insurance company holds them. The annuity contract also specifies the interest rate that the insurance company will pay on the accumulated funds. A specific interest rate may be guaranteed for one or two years and sometimes as long as five years. After the guaranteed-rate period expires, the contract may call for the rate to be reviewed at specified intervals, such as quarterly or annually. At that time, the insurance company adjusts the rate in accordance with changes in the general interest rates. Many insurance companies use the rate paid on Treasury bills as an index for setting the rate paid on annuities. Sometimes they use indexes such as consumer prices or cost-of-living calculations. Most insurance companies also guarantee that the interest rate paid on annuities will never be lower than a particular rate specified in the contract (usually 4%). When an insurance company receives premiums on a fixed annuity, it invests them along with other funds it holds.[1]

Taxes on the interest earned on annuity contracts are deferred and are paid when distribution of the funds takes place. For this reason, this product is often referred to as a tax-deferred annuity. In this book the shorter, generic term *annuity* is used.

The individual who purchases the annuity is referred to as the *owner*. The person who receives payments from the annuity is the *annuitant*. The annuitant may or may not be the contract owner. Each of these terms will become more meaningful as you learn more about annuities.

TYPES OF ANNUITIES

To meet consumers' diverse resources and financial needs, various types of annuities exist. Two basic categories of annuities are immediate annuities and deferred annuities. These types differ in the time that payments to the annuitant begin.

Immediate Annuities

An *immediate annuity* provides for payments to commence shortly after the purchase date according to an agreed-upon schedule of monthly, quarterly, semiannual or annual payments. For example, a retiree who sells her home may use the sale proceeds to purchase an immediate annuity. This annuity will provide her with immediate, regular income for a specified number of years or for the rest of her life, depending on other provisions in the annuity contract.

Deferred Annuities

With a *deferred annuity*, the contract specifies a future date that payments to the annuitant will begin. This date is referred to as the *maturity date*.

The period before the maturity date on a deferred annuity is sometimes called the *accumulation period*. The period following the maturity date during which payments are made to the annuitant is known as the *liquidation* or *distribution period*. As with immediate annuities, the annuitant will receive payments according to the schedule in the contract.

To understand how a deferred annuity is commonly used, consider a middle-aged man who wishes to provide for economic security during his retirement years. While he expects to receive a regular income from Social Security and from his company's pension plan, he believes he will need an additional source of income in order to live in the manner he desires. He could contract for a deferred annuity that will begin providing him with a regular income when he reaches age 65. He could purchase this annuity with a lump sum payment or with regularly scheduled payments made until the benefits are scheduled to begin.

COMMON VARIATIONS IN CONTRACT TERMS

Once a consumer decides on the type of annuity, other decisions must be made. Four of the contract terms for which options generally are available are frequency of premiums, methods of payout to annuitants (settlement options), number of lives covered by the contract and terms by which the owner can terminate the contract before maturity (surrender terms).

Premium Options

Premiums for annuities are usually paid in one of three ways. In the first method, the customer pays a single, lump sum premium when the contract is signed. For example, an individual may purchase an annuity with a single payment of $10,000, $50,000 or any other minimum amount that the insurance company will accept. Lump sum premiums can be paid for either immediate annuities or deferred annuities.

The second method is available only for deferred annuities. In this option, the customer pays premiums on a regular schedule (annual, semi-annual, quarterly or monthly) until the date on which benefit payments begin. Some individuals choose this option because it is similar to making regular deposits in a savings account—a comfortable, familiar habit.

The third option, which also applies to deferred annuities only, is the flexible premium annuity. This feature permits flexibility in the timing and amount of premium payments. The flexible premium annuity often is attractive to individuals who want a program in which they can vary the amounts they save each year. People who earn commissions or other types of irregular income and families with growing children are two examples of customers who may be interested in a product with this type of flexibility.

For example, contract terms of a typical flexible premium annuity may require an initial minimum deposit of $2,500. The contract remains in effect and the funds that already have been paid in continue to accrue interest even if the annuity owner does not wish to pay into the annuity on a regular schedule.[2]

Settlement Options

Settlement options refer to the various ways that funds from an annuity will be distributed. The insurance company and the annuity owner agree to settlement terms when the owner wishes to begin receiving income from the annuity. Four major types of settlement options are commonly available.

First, the settlement may be made in a single lump sum. This lump sum includes both the amount the owner paid in premiums and the interest the funds have earned. Second, the owner may decide to receive interest-only payments until a later date on which another settlement option will take effect. Third, the owner may elect to have the settlement paid in a specified number or designated dollar amount of payments over a number of years. For example, the annuitant could receive quarterly checks for equal amounts over a ten-year period.

The fourth settlement option—the life income option—is perhaps the one most commonly associated with annuities. With the life option, the annuitant receives payments until he or she dies. Payments may or may not continue after the annuitant's death. Three life income options are straight life, period certain and refund.

Straight Life

A *straight life annuity* contract provides for guaranteed periodic payments that terminate upon the annuitant's death. No remaining balance is paid to a beneficiary or to the annuitant's estate after the annuitant dies.

To understand how a straight life annuity works, consider the case of Lee Smith, who sev-

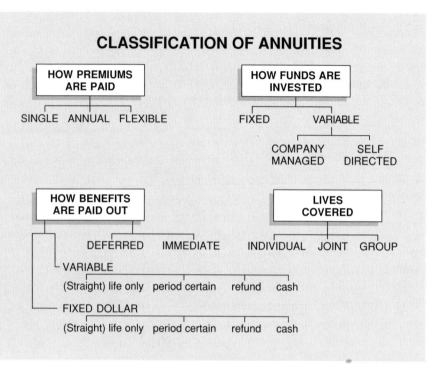

CLASSIFICATION OF ANNUITIES

HOW PREMIUMS ARE PAID

SINGLE   ANNUAL   FLEXIBLE

HOW FUNDS ARE INVESTED

FIXED   VARIABLE

COMPANY   SELF
MANAGED   DIRECTED

HOW BENEFITS ARE PAID OUT

DEFERRED   IMMEDIATE

VARIABLE

(Straight) life only   period certain   refund   cash

FIXED DOLLAR

(Straight) life only   period certain   refund   cash

LIVES COVERED

INDIVIDUAL   JOINT   GROUP

eral years ago purchased a straight life deferred annuity that would begin providing him with a regular income when he reached age 65. Lee lived until age 87 and received annuity payments until his death. Once he died, payments ceased. Had he died at age 67, the insurance company that had sold him the annuity would have stopped payments at that time. Had he lived to age 100 or more, the company would have made payments to him until then.

The straight life annuity option, therefore, does not guarantee that the annuitant will receive payments equal to the amount paid as premiums on the contract.[3] Because this option limits potential payouts, insurance companies offer a higher return for it than for some other plans, such as those described next. Overall, the straight life annuity option provides the maximum income per dollar of outlay compared to other annuity options.

Period Certain and Refund Options

Some individuals do not want to use the duration of their lives as the factor that determines whether they will profit, break even or perhaps even lose money on their investments. Straight life annuities therefore do not appeal to them. Instead, these individuals often choose annuities with period certain or refund options.

Period certain and refund options guarantee a minimum amount that the insurance company will pay on an annuity. Both of these options can be regarded as types of death benefits, since they provide for a payment to be made to designated beneficiaries upon the annuitant's death. Because they provide added benefits for the consumer and create additional costs for the insurance company, annuities with period certain and refund options offer the consumer lower income per premium dollar than do straight life annuities.

Period Certain   *Period certain* refers to a guarantee from the insurance company that it will make annuity payments to a beneficiary for a specific number of years even if the annuitant dies before the end of this period. However, payments to the annuitant will continue as long as he or she lives.

Since a period certain option of a fixed annuity may be selected at the same time that other settlement agreements (such as the amount and frequency of payments) are determined, it guarantees that a specific sum will be paid out by the company. For example, consider a life annuity with a five-year period certain option. If the an-

nuitant dies during the third year of the liquidation period, the insurance company will continue to make payments to the annuitant's
beneficiary for the next two years. If the annuity
pays out $4,000 each quarter ($16,000 a year), a
five-year period certain guarantees that $80,000
will actually be paid out.[4] If the annuitant survives the first five years of the liquidation period,
the annuity will continue to be paid out in the
normal manner, ceasing upon the annuitant's
death.

Refund Option   The *refund option* is another
form of guarantee offered by insurance companies. This option provides that in the event of the
annuitant's death, the company will pay out an
amount at least equal to the total dollars paid in
as premiums. Since this is another form of life
income option, the company will, of course, continue to pay the guaranteed amount of monthly
income for as long as the annuitant lives.

Refund options can be classified into two basic
types. With a *cash refund*, the insurance company
agrees that if the annuitant dies, it will refund in
cash the difference between the income the annuitant received and the amount paid in premiums plus interest earned. With an *installment refund*, the insurance company agrees to continue
to make periodic payments to the annuitant's
beneficiary until the total of the payments made
to the annuitant and to the beneficiary equals the
amount the owner paid for the annuity contract
plus interest earned. The longer the payout is to
continue after the annuitant's death, the smaller
will be the periodic payments.

Refund and period certain options offer benefits to a consumer who is reluctant to invest a
substantial amount of money in a product whose

return depends solely on the length of his or her life. At the same time, not all annuity purchasers favor refund options. The main reason is money—annuities with refund options pay annuitants lower amounts of income than do comparable contracts without them. The refund option represents an extra benefit for the contract owner and an extra cost for the insurance company.

Number of Annuitants

An annuity contract may be written to provide for one or more annuitants. If only one annuitant is named, the insurance company agrees to provide that person with income beginning on a specific date and continuing for an agreed-upon period—usually the duration of the individual's life.

Some contracts cover more than one person. One widely used contract of this type is the *joint and survivor annuity*. Under this arrangement, two people are insured, usually husband and wife. Beginning on the date set in the contract, payments are paid to the annuitants. Payments are guaranteed to continue to the surviving spouse upon the other spouse's death. Depending on the contract terms, the continuing payments will either be in the same amount as when both annuitants were alive or be reduced.

Two types of joint and survivor annuities are commonly used. With a joint and two-thirds survivor option, the surviving spouse receives two-thirds of the income paid to the original annuitant. With a joint and one-half option, the surviving spouse receives half of that income.

Surrender Terms

Another set of annuity contract terms important to an investor are the surrender charges. The word *surrender* describes the termination of an insurance contract, such as an annuity, by the owner. When an individual surrenders a contract, he or she turns in to the insurance company the documents stating the contract terms. In return, the company gives the owner a sum of money known as the *surrender value*.

Surrender value is the cash sum that the insurance company agrees to pay the owner in the event the owner surrenders the policy prior to maturity. The surrender value of a policy increases in proportion to the number of premiums paid, but it does not always equal the amount that the contract owner has paid. The surrender value may be lower than the total premium amount, because under some circumstances insurance companies impose surrender charges. Although surrender charges vary among insurance companies, most annuities stipulate a period of about seven years during which some penalty is imposed.

Surrender charges are one reason that consumers should not attempt to use annuities as short-term, liquid investments as they might deposit accounts. Some annuity contracts offer loan privileges whereby the policy owner may borrow against the contract rather than accept a distribution of cash. This may be advantageous in some cases; however, the loans carry interest charges that vary according to company regulations. Furthermore, a policy loan is considered taxable income.

MATHEMATICAL BASIS OF FIXED ANNUITIES

How do annuities work? How can a company afford to pay an individual a guaranteed income for life, particularly when that income exceeds the total amount of premiums plus interest that have accrued in the contract? The answer is that an annuity is an insurance product and, as such, provides a life insurance benefit to *annuitants*. The cost of the benefit is included in the premium paid for the annuity.

Insurance companies use demographic projections and complex mathematical calculations to develop and price the annuity products they sell. A company must use projections on average life expectancies when it prices its products, because the number of years people will live directly relates to the amount that the company pays out on its annuities. In turn, statistical projections on the average number of people who will die at different ages influence the amount a policy owner must pay for an annuity.

Mortality Tables

One important mathematical device insurance companies use for pricing annuities is a mortality table. A *mortality table* is a mathematical tool used to calculate the frequency of deaths that will occur between successive birthdays among a group of people who were born during the same calendar year. The numbers in a mortality table are calculated through the use of *probabilities*—mathematical equations that express the likelihood of the occurrence of a specific event. Mortality tables are developed by *actuaries*—insurance specialists who are experts in mathematics. Actuaries calculate risks, premiums, reserves and other mathematical factors for insurance companies.

Figure 3-1 presents a portion of a mortality table currently in use. According to this table, out of 100,000 people born during the same year, only

FIGURE 3-1
Annuity Mortality Table, 1983 Table Male

Age	Number of Deaths per 1,000	Age	Number of Deaths per 1,000
0	0.0000	44	2.1290
1	0.0000	45	2.3990
2	0.0000	46	2.6930
3	0.0000	47	3.0090
4	0.0000	48	3.3430
5	0.3770	49	3.6940
6	0.3500	50	4.0570
7	0.3330	51	4.4310
8	0.3520	52	4.8120
9	0.3680	53	5.1980
10	0.3820	54	5.5910
11	0.3940	55	5.9940
12	0.4050	56	6.4090
13	0.4150	57	6.8390
14	0.4250	58	7.2900
15	0.4350	59	7.7820
16	0.4460	60	8.3380
17	0.4580	61	8.9830
18	0.4720	62	9.7400
19	0.4880	63	10.6300
20	0.5050	64	11.6640
21	0.5250	65	12.0510
22	0.5460	66	14.1990
23	0.5700	67	15.7170
24	0.5960	68	17.4140
25	0.6220	69	19.2960
26	0.6500	70	21.3710
27	0.6770	71	23.6470
28	0.7040	72	26.1310
29	0.7310	73	28.8350
30	0.7590	74	31.7940
31	0.7860	75	35.0460
32	0.8140	76	38.6310
33	0.8430	77	42.5870
34	0.8760	78	46.9510
35	0.9170	79	51.7550
36	0.9680	80	57.0260
37	1.0320	81	62.7910
38	1.1140	82	69.0810
39	1.2160	83	75.9080
40	1.3410	84	83.2300
41	1.4920	85	90.9870
42	1.6730	86	99.1220
43	1.8860	87	107.5770

FIGURE 3-1 Continued

Age	Number of Deaths per 1,000	Age	Number of Deaths per 1,000
88	116.3160	102	315.8260
89	125.3940	103	342.3770
90	134.8870	104	372.8860
91	144.8730	105	405.2780
92	155.4290	106	442.2770
93	166.6290	107	483.4060
94	178.5370	108	528.9890
95	191.2140	109	579.3510
96	204.7210	110	634.8140
97	219.1200	111	695.7040
98	234.7350	112	762.3430
99	251.8890	113	835.0560
100	270.9060	114	914.1670
101	292.1110	115	1000.0000

* At age 115, all 1,000 have died; at age 114, 914 have died; etc

Source: Kemper Investors' Life Insurance Company

87,149 will be alive when they reach age 65. Out of that group, 1,348 will probably die during the following year, leaving only 85,801 survivors. The mortality table is constructed so that all of the original 100,000 will have died by age 115.

The numbers in the mortality table allow an insurance company to project its likely future obligations to annuitants. Similarly, the company uses the mortality table to project how many dollars will be released to it by annuitants who die. This information, together with statistics the company gathers on the interest it can earn on its holdings plus predictions of operating costs, is then used to calculate the premiums to be charged for annuities and other products.

Example of Annuity Pricing

To learn more about how insurance companies use various factors to determine premium costs, consider the example of a brother and sister who both wish to purchase straight life fixed annuities. Both want an annuity that will pay $1,000 a year for the rest of their lives. The brother is 65 years old, and the sister is 66.

When the brother and sister meet with the insurance company representative who sells annuities, they learn that the brother's annuity can be purchased for a single premium of $9,178 and the sister's for $8,890. During the discussion, they learn that the insurance company is basing its calculations on an earned interest rate of 8%.

As the brother and sister ponder the offer, they try to determine how the insurance company developed those two figures. Here is their calculation:

Cost of annuity at age 65 is	$9,178
Cost of annuity at age 66 is	−8,980
	$ 198

The difference between the two annuities is $198. They therefore figure that $198 of principal is liquidated in year 1. But they know that since an annuitant would receive $1,000 during the first year, they must do more figuring to determine how the company can afford to pay that money. It must be interest, they decide. At 8% interest, $9,178 will earn 734.24 in one year:

$$\$734.24 + \$198.00 = \$932.24$$

But $932.24 is $67.76 less than $1,000. How, they wonder, can the insurance company promise to pay the annuitant $1,000 each year if the payment exceeds the amount by which the annuitant's capital decreases plus the interest that the capital would have earned? Furthermore, won't the interest the annuity funds earn decrease each year as the capital is liquidated? How, then, could the company continue to pay them each $1,000 a year if they lived until age 90 or even older?

Questions like these are typical of those posed by individuals who are familiar with certificates of deposit and other savings products. These individuals are most familiar with arrangements in which their accounts remain independent of other people's and the value of the accounts decreases as funds are withdrawn.

In contrast to deposit products, annuities are calculated based on the participation of many people. Thus, when the brother and sister begin receiving income from their annuities, that money will come from a pooled fund that provides an insurance benefit to annuitants who live long enough to collect it. The $67.76 missing from the above figures represents the insurance benefit that annuitants who survive to age 66 will receive. The insurance company calculated that figure based on the number of annuitants who are likely to die during the year. Therefore, the death benefit to surviving annuitants will grow larger each year during the liquidation period. If the annuitant lives long enough, both principal and interest eventually will be exhausted. When that occurs, the entire payment will come from the insurance benefit.

INVESTOR CONSIDERATIONS

The promise of a guaranteed lifetime income during retirement is attractive to many investors. But a guaranteed income is only one factor that investors must take into account when considering annuities. Among the other issues that should be examined are risk, liquidity, earnings and taxes.

Risk

Annuities are relatively safe investments. While they are not covered by federal deposit insurance, the principal and interest an individual invests in a fixed annuity contract are protected by the rigid state and federal regulations that govern insurance companies' operations. Yet these regulations do not protect an investor from all potential problems. If the insurance company that sold an annuity to an individual experiences severe business problems and becomes insolvent, other insurance companies doing business in the same state will be required to help meet that company's remaining obligations. However, the annuitant may face extra paperwork and delays in attempting to obtain funds. Therefore, it is a good idea to research the soundness of the insurance company before purchasing an annuity from it. One way to do this is to use *Best's Insurance Reports,* a publication that reports on and rates the financial strength of life insurance companies.

While the dollars that an individual invests in and earns through an annuity are relatively safe, the annuitant is not protected from purchasing power risk (see Chapter 1). The fixed income received from an annuity loses its value in times of inflation. For example, while a monthly income of $1,000 may sound adequate to an individual in 1990, that amount may seem trivial in 2010 if inflation has greatly increased the cost of living. Since many investors purchase annuities to provide for living expenses during their retirement, the possibility of decreased purchasing power is an important consideration.

Liquidity

Annuities are relatively liquid investments because they provide ways for individuals to surrender their contracts and withdraw their funds during the accumulation period. They are not completely liquid, however, because investors may not receive the full amount that they have paid in as premiums if they decide to withdraw from their annuities. The amount that an individual would lose depends on the surrender fees and penalties assessed by the insurance company. These charges are described in the annuity contract.

Earnings

Interest earnings on annuities have attracted many current investors. Rates in the last few years have been competitive, generally paying somewhat more than typical CDs.

Guarantee periods vary with different insurance companies. Some will pay an initial rate for one or two years followed by subsequent annual guarantees. Others will peg their rates to formulas based on Treasury bill or consumer price indexes.

A desirable feature that a discerning buyer will seek in an annuity is the bail out provision. With this provision, the contract owner may bail out without paying any surrender charge if the rate falls below a certain designated percentage from the original rate, even if the initial guarantee period has expired.

For example, assume the initial guaranteed rate is 8% for a period of one year. The contract promises a 1½% bail out provision. The contract also says that a surrender charge is made upon a premature withdrawal anytime within seven years from the purchase date. After the initial one-year period of the contract, the company announces the next year's interest rate will be 6¼%. Since this rate dropped over 1½% from the initial rate, the customer is entitled to avoid any surrender charges if the contract is cashed in.

Income Tax

One of the main appeals of deferred annuities is the income tax advantages they offer investors. Investors pay no taxes on the earnings during the accumulation period; taxes are deferred until the liquidation period. Once payouts to the annuitant begin, only a portion of each payment is taxed as income. The remaining portion, which is not subject to income taxes, is considered as a return of the money that the investor paid into the annuity during the accumulation period.

The portion of an annuitant's income that is subject to taxes is determined through a calculation required by the U.S. Department of the Treasury. This complex calculation is based on the projection of the amount the annuitant will receive in annuity income if he or she lives to life expectancy. This total income is referred to as the *expected return*. Once an expected return is determined, the next step is to calculate the percentage of the amount that was invested in the contract. For example, if an investor paid $120,000 for an annuity and his or her expected return is $200,000, 60% of the expected return represents money that was paid for the annuity. Once this percentage is calculated, it is used each year to determine how much of the annual annuity income should be considered return of capital and how much should be regarded as taxable income. Using the above example, 40% of the investor's annual annuity income would be considered reportable income.

The Tax Reform Act of 1986 added some income tax penalties to annuities. One important addition was a 10% penalty applying to lump sum withdrawals from annuities before age 59½. This penalty applies whether the amount is taken as a loan or an outright withdrawal.[5]

While annuities retained their general tax deferral benefits under the new law, an important exception was made in the case of business-owned annuities. If a business entity, such as a corporation, partnership, or trust, owns an annuity on an employee's life, any interest earnings or annual gains in the contract are subject to current income taxes. Annuities that are part of qualified plans, such as pensions and similar employee benefit programs, are exempt from this ruling. Immediate annuities are also exempt.[6]

FOOTNOTES

[1]Not all of the dollars a contract owner pays are invested, since some are used for sales commissions and fees. These charges differ among companies and among contracts. (Some companies have no charges other than surrender fees.) However, should the insured die before the cash value stated in the contract equals the amount of premiums paid in, most contracts provide for a payment to the beneficiary of at least the amounts paid in, regardless of sales charges.

[2]These contract provisions appear in the "Advantage III" (flexible premium deferred annuity, Kemper Investors Life Insurance Company, Chicago, IL).

[3]In the event of the contract owner's death during the accumulation period, the proceeds will revert to the beneficiary. If no beneficiary has been named, proceeds will revert to the annuitant's estate.

[4]It is common for insurance companies to pay the present value of the remaining payments in a lump sum to the beneficiary rather than continuing the payments until the end of the certain period.

[5]There is an exemption to this 10% penalty if the amount of withdrawals before age 59½ is part of a series of approximately equal periodic payments over a lifetime. Also exempt are such payments in the event of death or disability.

[6]In addition to employer pension plans, the exclusion of taxable earnings on annuities applies to IRAs and 403(b) tax-sheltered annuities sponsored by certain nonprofit corporate employers.

4

CHAPTER FOUR

VARIABLE
ANNUITIES

- Structure of the variable annuity

- Forms of variable annuity contracts

- Calculation of values of variable annuities

- Performance history of variable annuities and their effectiveness as a financial planning tool

- Investor considerations in purchasing variable annuities

F OR MANY YEARS, marketers of annuity products, along with savings institutions, emphasized the advantages of conservative and secure investments. During the 1930s, when the U.S. economy was experiencing only moderate inflation rates, many people purchased annuities for retirement in the belief that they ensured a comfortable, guaranteed income for life. A successful insurance company advertisement of the late 1930s enthusiastically proclaimed, "Retire for life on 300 dollars a month!"

Then rising inflation rates began to affect the average person's standard of living. Beginning in the 1960s, people became aware that they had to plan for more retirement dollars just to keep pace with anticipated increases in living costs. Savers sought financial instruments that could more readily keep up with inflation. Individuals of even average means were turning to the stock market for an increasing portion of their investments.

Like savings institutions, insurance companies looked for ways to improve their traditional products. In an attempt to combine traditional annuity guarantees with the growth potential of a securities investment, they developed the variable annuity.

CHARACTERISTICS OF VARIABLE ANNUITIES

To understand the structure of the *variable annuity*, compare it to the fixed annuity described in Chapter 3. Like the fixed annuity, the variable annuity is a contract between an individual and a life insurance company. With both types, the owner contributes premiums that, along with their earnings, are accumulated within the policy contract. At an agreed-upon time, the insurance company begins making payments to the annuitant. Payments are made over the individual's lifetime or for some other stipulated period.

The basic difference between fixed annuities and variable annuities is the way in which accumulated funds are invested and the resulting payout.[1] With fixed annuities, the accumulated funds are comingled with the insurance company's general investments. These investments help form the basis for the guaranteed cash values of life insurance and conventional annuity contracts. In general, insurance companies invest funds for their fixed products in long-term bonds and other nonspeculative issues.

In contrast, the premium payments made on a variable annuity are not combined with the insurance company's general investments; instead, they are placed in stocks, government securities and other types of fluctuating investments. These investments have more growth potential than those that underlie fixed annuities, but the variable annuity investments also are subject to a greater degree of risk. The investments make up a portfolio that is managed in much the same way as a typical mutual fund.

TYPES OF VARIABLE ANNUITIES

Variable annuities generally are divided into two basic types. The difference between them lies in who has control over investing the money deposited into the annuity. With the first type, the *company-managed variable annuity*, the insurance company determines how the annuity funds are invested. With the second type, which could be referred to as a *self-directed variable annuity*, the annuity owner has substantial control over the investment of funds.

Company-Managed Variable Annuity

The original variable annuities, introduced in the 1950s, were company-managed types. In this type of annuity, premiums paid in by contract owners are pooled and placed in what the insurance company designates as a separate account. This method serves to distinguish these investments from the company's other invested funds.[2] The account is organized like a mutual fund in that it is made up of various investments—usually stocks, bonds and government securities. The insurance companies' investment managers buy and sell these investments on a continuing basis.

Like mutual fund managers, the insurance company tries to invest the money wisely and profitably so that it will generate a competitive return for its investors. In addition, the insurance company must meet both state and federal regulations regarding investment practices for these products.[3]

One of the better known company-managed variable annuities is the College Retirement and Equities Fund, or CREF. Designed by the Teacher's Annuity and Insurance Association, it was the first variable annuity, appearing on the market in 1952. Because of CREF's relatively long history, it has been the subject of many detailed studies. (The CREF annuity is treated in greater detail later in the chapter.)

An example of a hypothetical company-managed variable annuity is illustrated in Figure 4-1. The investment portfolio for this annuity

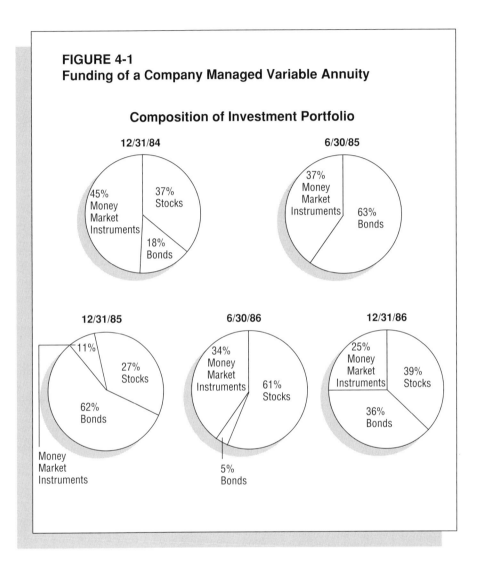

FIGURE 4-1
Funding of a Company Managed Variable Annuity

Composition of Investment Portfolio

12/31/84

45% Money Market Instruments
37% Stocks
18% Bonds

6/30/85

37% Money Market Instruments
63% Bonds

12/31/85

11%
27% Stocks
62% Bonds
Money Market Instruments

6/30/86

34% Money Market Instruments
61% Stocks
5% Bonds

12/31/86

25% Money Market Instruments
39% Stocks
36% Bonds

consists of a combination of stocks, bonds and money market instruments. Note that at different times, the insurance company's investment managers varied the mix of investments based on the perceived market potential for each type of investment used in the plan. For example, on December 31, 1984, the mix was 37% stocks, 18%

bonds and 45% money market instruments. The
fund managers decided that by June 30, 1985,
they would sell all the stocks and switch to bonds
(63%) and money market instruments (37%). By
the concluding period, the fund consisted of a
fairly balanced mix of 39% stocks, 36% bonds
and 25% money market instruments.

The above sequence of investment decisions
demonstrates the continuous management of assets placed in variable annuity funds. Investment
managers consider various economic indicators in
making decisions that they believe are timely and
will lead to maximum profits.

Self-Directed Variable Annuity

With the self-directed variable annuity, the contract owner can choose from several investments,
each with different objectives. The selection of
investments may be made during both the accumulation and distribution periods. In effect, the
contract owner may construct a personal investment portfolio within the annuity. The owner se-
lects investments based on his or her investment
objectives in much the same way that a mutual
fund investor does (see Chapter 2).

Choosing an Annuity Investment Portfolio

The annuity application form lists the selection
of investments that the insurance company offers.
Figure 4-2 shows five selections available for a
hypothetical self-directed variable annuity. These
include four mutual funds with differing objectives, plus a fixed account. The *fixed account* offers
guaranteed safety of principal and specifies a fixed
interest rate.[4] Customers choose from among these
options according to their investment objectives.

FIGURE 4-2
Investment Options in a Hypothetical Self-Directed Variable Annuity

1
FIXED ACCOUNT
Guaranteed Interest Rate
Guaranteed Safety of Principal

2
EMERGING GROWTH FUND
Composed primarily of common stocks of emerging growth companies with potential for long-term capital growth

3
GROWTH STOCK FUND
Objective is long-term growth of capital and future income rather than current income; investments are in common stock of companies with good growth histories

4
CASH MANAGEMENT FUND
Mainly U.S. government securities; objectives are preservation of capital, current income and liquidity

5
FINANCIAL BOND FUND
Composed of high-grade bonds; objectives are high-yield current income and preservation of capital

CONTRACT STIPULATIONS
Any percentage combination of options may be selected.
Transfers among funds may be made up to eight times a year free of charge.
Transfers may be made free of charge from the variable account to the fixed account, or from the fixed account to the variable account as long as the minimum amount transferred is at least $1,000.
Such transfers are permitted only once a year.
No sales charge may be deducted from contributions.
Full or partial withdrawals may be made at any time. Contributions that have been on deposit for five years may be withdrawn free of charge.
Flexibility of investment designation remains after annuity payments begin-changes among variable accounts may be made up to four times per year.
Beneficiary is guaranteed the greater of the account's value or 100% of total contributions.
Initial minimum payment is $25. Subsequent minimum payments are $25.
At least $300 must be deposited during the year.

On the annuity application the customer indicates, usually in percentage units, how each premium is to be allocated among the selected accounts. Most contracts allow an unlimited number of percentage combinations. The applicant can even allocate the entire premium to a single investment choice.

Changing the Investment Mix

One distinguishing characteristic of self-directed annuities is the owner's ability to change the composition of the annuity portfolio. Three major factors that affect how individuals invest their assets are their investment objectives and philosophies, their financial standing and economic conditions. Since each of these factors may change over time, it is advantageous to the investor to be able to change the way in which his or her money is invested.

As an individual progresses through life, his or her investment philosophy and objectives often change. Many people who previously might have been inclined to take investment risks may become more cautious as they grow older. For the owner of a variable annuity, a change to more conservative investments may mean moving money from stock funds to funds composed of government securities or even to a fixed fund. The typical self-directed variable annuity offers the contract owner the opportunity to redirect the investment of funds as his or her investment objectives change.

The hypothetical self-directed annuity in Figure 4-2 illustrates this benefit. The "contract stipulation" portion of the figure describes some of the rules governing the transfer of funds. Note that the contract owner is permitted to make transfers up to eight times a year among the variable account options. The owner may also make transfers to and from a fixed account.[5] These rules provide ample opportunity for changes in investment directions.

Changes in one's financial standing may also alter an individual's willingness to accept risks. For example, some individuals may invest in more aggressive and riskier funds only after they have accumulated what they consider an adequate nest egg. Similarly, some individuals move their variable annuity funds into conservative options if they experience losses in their other investments.

Economic conditions and forecasts may also lead an individual to take advantage of a variable annuity's flexibility. When stock prices are expected to fall, some individuals direct their money out of stock funds and into other types of funds. When yields on other investments are falling, investors often move their money into bond funds because these generally are considered good investments during such periods. Thus, variable annuities allow the investor to react in the face of changing market conditions.

Examples of Self-Directed Plans
To better understand the implications of investment choices in a self-directed plan, look at some hypothetical investors and their choice of investment mix from the options outlined in Figure 4-2.

> Ruth Radcliffe, age 25, "promotable" executive
> Investment mix: 60% option 2, Emerging Growth Fund; 40% option 3, Growth Stock Fund.

Ruth figures that she can invest in these rather speculative funds because if she makes some incorrect decisions and sustains some losses, she has plenty of remaining years in which to deposit additional funds and still accumulate an ample

nest egg. Also, as Ruth grows older, she may become more conservative with her investment
choices and less inclined to speculate.

> Charlie Vandermeer, age 55, university professor
> Investment mix: 50% option 5, Financial Bond
> Fund; 40% option 4, Cash Management Fund; 10%
> option 3, the Growth Stock Fund.

Charlie's rationale for these relatively conservative choices is that he wants to be on the safe
side—that is, accumulate as much as possible and
expose only a small portion of his investment to
risk. Perhaps at an earlier age he would have in-
dulged in greater speculation, but now it seems
wiser to be more conservative.

> Frank Nelson, age 66, retired
> Investment mix: 50% option 1, Fixed Account; 50%
> option 5, the Financial Bond Fund.

Now that Frank is retired and receiving his lifetime payments, he wants to ensure a steady flow
of income. He has split his choice right down the
middle: half in the fixed account, with its designated interest rate and guaranteed safety of principal, and half in the bond fund, with its high
current income yield and emphasis on capital
preservation. Barring any drastic changes in the
economy, Frank will probably continue to rely on
this investment selection for his annuity income.

COMPUTATION OF ANNUITY ACCUMULATIONS
AND PAYMENTS

Owners of variable annuities receive regular
statements on the value of their investment accounts. Like CD owners and other investment

holders, annuity owners want to know the current values of their holdings.

Computing the value at any given time of a variable annuity contract can be complex. With a variable annuity, one is dealing with fluctuating stock market investments. The process therefore is more complicated than calculating the value of a CD, which has a guaranteed interest rate over a specified time period.

Most insurance companies have adopted a unit method of expressing annuity values. Generally, two types of units form the variable annuity contract. These units correspond to the two basic time classifications for annuities: the period during which dollars are being accumulated (accumulation period) and the period in which the insurance company makes the annuity payments (distribution period).

Accumulation Units

During the years in which premiums are paid into the contract, the annuity owner acquires accumulation units. Accumulation units have a designated initial price at the time of the annuity purchase but fluctuate in value thereafter. In the case of company-managed products, the changing values will correspond to the performance of the pool of investments. This is similar to the way mutual fund values are expressed. As described in Chapter 2, a mutual fund is described in terms of shares. Like a mutual fund share, each accumulation unit of a variable annuity has a designated value on a given day. In the case of self-directed annuities, the values of the fund or combination of funds the policy owner has chosen are totaled. The value of each accumulation unit is then calculated from this total.

Under both company-managed and self-directed plans, each premium payment purchases a certain number of accumulation units. The number of units varies according to the unit's current market values. The number of units continues to increase, as additional purchases are made, although each unit's value will vary over the life of the contract according to the worth in the marketplace. This, too, is similar to the manner in which mutual fund share values are calculated.

The following example illustrates how this works out in practice:

Initial Value of Accumulation Unit on January 1	$ 5.00
Monthly Premium Payment	100.00
Initial Number of Units Purchased	20

Subsequent Accumulation	*Unit Values*	*Number of Units Purchased*
February 1	$5.05	19.80
March 1	4.87	20.53
April 1	4.94	20.24
May 1	4.99	20.04
June 1	5.12	19.53

At the end of the six-month period, the owner will have a total of 120.14 accumulation units. As stated above, the value of these units will continue to fluctuate according to the units' market value. With each premium payment, the contract owner adds to the total of accumulation units. The accumulation unit price will probably continue to fluctuate. When the annuity matures, the contract owner will have been credited with a specified number of accumulation units.

Annuity Units

In order for the insurance company to begin paying out income from the annuity, accumulation units are converted into annuity units. An *annuity unit* is a measure of value that an insurance company uses when it calculates the amount of income to be paid to an annuitant. At retirement, the annuitant is credited with a designated number of annuity units.

The exact number of annuity units to be credited depends on four basic factors. One is the annuitant's age. As described in Chapter 3, the insurance company calculates from its mortality tables the charge to make in order to provide a designated amount of lifetime income at a specified age. The second factor is the number of guaranteed payments. If the annuitant chooses a period certain life income option, the extra charge for that benefit will be reflected in the calculation of the annuity unit.[6] The third factor is the interest rate that the insurance company projects. If the company predicts a fairly high interest rate, the annuity unit will have a greater value than it would with a lower rate. Interest rates typically are projected annually to determine the projected investment return. Finally, there are administrative expenses to be incorporated into the unit cost calculations.

All of these factors affect the number of annuity units credited to the contract owner. Of course, the charges vary from company to company.

Fluctuating Value of Annuity Units

The calculated number of annuity units remains constant over the payment period. The annuitant has the option of choosing a fixed or a variable payment or, as is often the case, a combination of both. With the variable payout, the annuity unit's value may fluctuate just as it does during the accumulation period. The value will continue to vary according to the performance of the underlying investment portfolio and the general administrative costs that the company incurs. Obviously, the amount of periodic income also will fluctuate.

For example, suppose that on January 1, the date the annuitant retires, he or she has collected a total of 10,000 accumulation units. Assume further that at that time the 10,000 units have a market value of $50,000 (of course, these are round-figures).

Using the above process, the insurance company then converts the annuitant's 10,000 accumulation units into 100 annuity units. On the day of the first payment, each annuity unit is worth $10.00. If the annuitant chooses the fixed payment option, the $1,000 monthly payment as listed in the example below as of January 1, would remain constant for the balance of the payout period. But assume that the annuitant chose a variable mode of payment. In that case a six-month projection of monthly payments would be as follows:

	Annuity Unit Value	Monthly Payment to Annuitant
January 1	$10.00	$1,000
February 1	10.17	1,017
March 1	9.73	973
April 1	9.89	989
May 1	10.11	1,011
June 1	10.57	1,057

There are two important reasons for the continued fluctuation in variable annuities after the retirement income period begins. The first is that the portfolio's value constantly changes to reflect current market conditions. The second is that the investments funding the annuity contract also change continually, just as they do during the accumulation period. The various stocks, bonds, and other financial instruments that make up the portfolio continue to be bought and sold. In a company-managed plan, the insurance company's investment managers continue to supervise this process. In a self-directed plan, the contract owner may frequently change the contents of the portfolio.

PERFORMANCE HISTORY OF THE VARIABLE ANNUITY

The initial objective of the variable annuity concept was to design a financial instrument that would combine the guaranteed features of annuities and the growth possibilities of equities. One popular theory was that the cost of living and common stock prices tend to move in the same direction over the long run. During the 1950s and 1960s, there did seem to be definite correlation between rising stock prices and the cost of living. However, a comparison of the consumer price index and Standard and Poor's index of 500 stocks from 1970 to 1987, as revealed in Chapter 1, shows wide fluctuation even during periods of accelerated inflation.

CREF Annuity

To see the relationship between cost-of-living changes and annuity unit values, consider the CREF annuity, introduced earlier in the chapter. Participants in the CREF annuity had ample reason to be disturbed when, beginning in 1973, the CREF annuity unit value dropped almost 40% in three years (see Figure 4-3). Consumer prices were

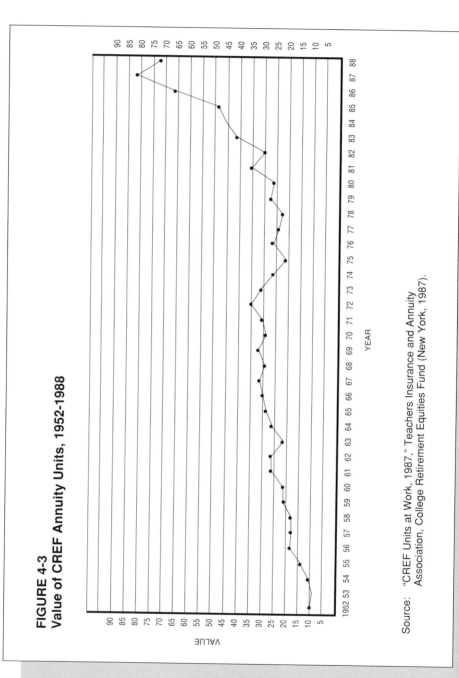

FIGURE 4-3
Value of CREF Annuity Units, 1952-1988

Source: "CREF Units at Work, 1987," Teachers Insurance and Annuity
Association, College Retirement Equities Fund (New York, 1987).

skyrocketing. Individuals who already had started drawing their annuity benefits saw their payments decrease while the cost of living increased.[7] Not only did this downturn affect retirees, but also those who were still investing for the future. The value of the accumulation units in annuity contracts dropped over 50% during that time. Therefore, even those who were still accumulating retirement funds were disappointed to learn that fund values did not appear to conform favorably to current economic conditions.

However, when computed over a longer time period, the CREF annuity unit value tended to increase along with the cost of living. From 1967 until 1987, the payout rate increased 385% during a period when the cost of living had risen 245.7%. While these data represent a close correlation between the rise in inflation and annuity payouts, certain other time periods did not show the same results. For example, between 1970 and 1983, the consumer price index increased each year. However, the value of the CREF annuity unit increased only during seven of those years. In total, while the consumer price index rose about 157%, the value of the CREF annuity unit increased only about 47%.

Some financial authorities have explained this phenomenon by proposing the existence of a definite relationship between inflation and stock prices. They point out that when prices rise rapidly, there is a corresponding increase in interest rates. When interest rates rise sharply, the stock market reacts by moving in the opposite direction. Therefore, when the cost of living takes a sudden jump, it seems that the value of the variable annuity unit tends to fall.

The variable annuity, therefore, did not always seem to provide the promised inflation

COMPANY MANAGED VARIABLE ANNUITY

This illustration shows the distribution of assets of the College Retirement Equities Fund, one of the major variable annuities.

As of December 31, 1987, total CREF investment portfolio assets were $25.4 billion.

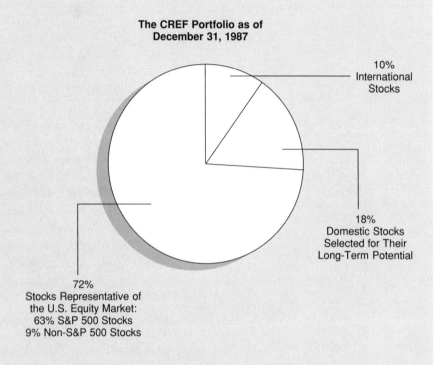

The CREF Portfolio as of December 31, 1987

10%
International
Stocks

18%
Domestic Stocks
Selected for Their
Long-Term Potential

72%
Stocks Representative of
the U.S. Equity Market:
63% S&P 500 Stocks
9% Non-S&P 500 Stocks

Source: "TIAA-CREF Annual Report, 1987" Teachers Insurance and Annuity Association College Retirement Equities Fund, New York, NY, 1988.

hedge, at least for CREF participants. In fairness it must be noted that other variable annuity companies were having similar experiences at the time. Proponents of the variable annuity, however, assert that they have never viewed this product as a temporary hedge against sudden inflation. To them, the variable annuity is based on the assumption of a long-term correlation between inflation and investment returns. If this principle is true, retired people in particular may find the variable annuity to be a favorable investment because it would allow them to enjoy a rise in income as the economy's productivity increases.

Despite the above setbacks, the variable annuity has achieved nationwide acceptance. The latest available figures indicate that as of the end of 1986 there were well over 4 million variable annuities in force with a value of more than $43 billion.[8]

INVESTOR CONSIDERATIONS IN PURCHASING VARIABLE ANNUITIES

The variable annuity, with its combination of traditional guarantees and investment flexibility, offers great promise as a financial planning tool. It has the potential to be more responsive to economic trends than the conventional savings account or even the traditional fixed annuity. However, the savings customer who has basically considered only fixed investments should be aware of the special concerns connected with the purchase of a variable annuity.

Risk

There are two important points to keep in mind regarding the risks of variable annuities. One concerns the insurance company that issues the annuity and the second the investment's fluctuating nature. Regarding the first point, it is essential to note that, while both fixed and variable annuities are marketed by savings institutions, neither product is covered by federal insuring agencies. The investment is backed only by the guarantees made by the insurance company that sells the annuity contract.

Although the insurance industry's record of financial stability has been very good, the annuity purchaser should investigate the company that issues the contract. While the savings institution marketing the annuity will have investigated the insurance company, the counselor must explain to the customer that government insurance does not apply to annuity products. In previous cases of insurance company failure, other insurance carriers have assumed the failed company's financial obligations. However, this process has entailed some delays. Further, although principal was safeguarded, the interest earnings promised in the original contract were not always credited to the customer.

The second area of risk—the fluctuating nature of the variable annuity—was discussed at length earlier in this chapter. Investors should recognize that whenever they place money in variable annuities, the dollar value of their investments is subject to both upward and downward change. An individual should assess his or her tolerance for risk when selecting a variable annuity and composing the annuity portfolio.

Particular caution is needed during the retirement period when the contract owner may be contemplating changing investment strategies. Many owners take a more conservative investment position at this time than when they were making deposits and accumulating funds. While it is possible to increase income payments by making the right investment choices, it is also possible to make the wrong decisions. Unlike during the accumulation period, when there is sufficient time to make up for a temporary loss, once retirement begins, it is difficult to recoup any losses resulting from investment mistakes.

Choosing an Annuity Type

Determining which type of variable annuity is suitable for an individual depends mainly on two factors. One is the potential purchaser's investment sophistication. The other is the extent to which the person wishes to become involved in investment decisions.

The first consideration applies to the inexperienced investor with limited knowledge of the stock market. In this case, a company-managed variable annuity is probably the better choice, since the insurance company will make all the investment choices and manage the portfolio.

The second factor concerns whether the contract owner wishes to continually monitor changing economic conditions and be responsible for changing the direction of investments in the annuity portfolio. With the self-directed type of variable annuity, the purchaser decides on the mix of investments in the portfolio. It is the contract owner's responsibility to periodically review these investments to see whether their performances are still in tune with his or her investment objectives and with changing economic conditions and to adjust the portfolio accordingly. The self-directed plan is probably more suited to an investor who is accustomed to making these types of decisions.

Insurance Company Charges

The investor should also be aware of the various charges that the insurance company's fund managers impose. Investment expertise is not offered free of charge. Each annuity contract has its own schedule of fees and other charges, and the investor should carefully assess these before making a purchase.

One charge that is commonly imposed is a surrender charge. This is similar to the surrender charge for fixed annuities described in Chapter 3. Typically, the surrender charge limits the amount of money that may be withdrawn during the early years of the contract. Some policies have a declining charge. For example, the charge might be 6% of the policy's total value in the first year and decreased by a percentage point each year. Thus, no surrender charge would be imposed on withdrawals made after the sixth year.

For funds invested in variable accounts, companies usually impose management charges. Fairly typical contract charges are $25 per year for administration plus an investment management fee of 1% or more of the variable account's total value. Funds held in a fixed account usually escape the investment management fees. The insurance company typically justifies these fees as providing for a guaranteed death benefit and covering the administrative expenses involved in providing a life income.

Income Tax Considerations

The income tax benefits of fixed annuities (see Chapter 3) also accrue to the owners of variable annuities. Under current law, income taxes are deferred until the contract owner withdraws funds from the annuity.

These tax laws give the variable annuity owner some definite tax advantages. For example, when a person invests in mutual funds, he or she must pay income tax on the yearly dividends and capital gains, even if the shareholder actually receives no payments during the year. Under the annuity "umbrella," on the other hand, the owner may invest in mutual funds and not be subject to income tax until any gain is actually paid out.

This income tax benefit is one of the major advantages of using a variable annuity contract to build up retirement funds. With a prudent investment policy that takes advantage of stock market conditions, an individual can create a nest egg of retirement income. Income taxes will not affect this personal fund during the accumulation period; it is only when money is drawn out that taxes become due. Further, when a person withdraws lifetime income from an annuity following retirement, he or she will probably be in a lower tax bracket than during the earning years.

FOOTNOTES

[1]Insurance companies often use the term *funded* or *funding* to describe the method of investment that characterizes the annuity contract, for example, "the contract is funded by a separate account invested in mutual funds and government securities."

[2]One advantage of a variable annuity is if the insurance company runs into financial problems, the funds in the separate account are beyond the reach of the company's creditors. This is also true for the portfolios in self-directed plans.

[3]Variable annuities are subject to regulation by the Securities and Exchange Commission, Internal Revenue Service, and state regulatory bodies.

[4]Interest rates on the fixed account may be guaranteed for periods ranging from one calendar quarter to one or two years or even longer.

[5]Note, however, that transfers from the funds to the fixed account, or the reverse are more limited than transfers among the funds.

[6]See Chapter 3, "Fixed Annuities," for a detailed description of life income options.

[7]CREF reevaluates its annuity value once each year and fixes its monthly payment amount for the following 12-month period. Many other variable annuity issuers pay a varying amount each month.

[8]Life Insurance Fact Book (Washington, DC: American Council of Life Insurance, 1986).

5

CHAPTER FIVE

LIFE INSURANCE FUNDAMENTALS

- Purposes of life insurance

- Life insurance policy provisions

- Elements of the single-premium life policy

- Uses of single-premium life insurance

- Investors' considerations in purchasing single-premium life insurance

Life insurance has long been regarded as an essential part of a family's basic financial planning. Most financial planners feel that the purchase of life insurance should be made before any major part of the family budget is allocated for other types of investments. The purpose of life insurance is to supply emergency funds and help continue family income in the event of a principal wage earner's death.

In recent years, however, insurance companies have begun developing improved investment features in life insurance products. For example, the single-premium life policy plan is being widely marketed by savings institutions as an investment comparable to annuities and certificates of deposit.

The counselor should be aware of the basic types of life insurance policies and how they fit in with the customer's personal financial planning. Another important point is the classification of life insurance as a legal contract, an aspect that is often overlooked. Still another consideration is the estate and tax issues that might arise when an individual receives the proceeds of a life insurance policy.

This chapter describes the purposes and the types of life insurance policies available, including various provisions of life insurance contracts. In addition, the chapter covers basic characteristics of the single-premium life contract and its applications in individual financial planning.

PURPOSES OF LIFE INSURANCE

Life insurance is based on the principle of the formation of a group of individuals who set aside funds that are pooled to provide a cash benefit for survivors when one group member dies. The original purpose of life insurance was to provide a modest death benefit for burial purposes. As the idea's popularity grew, life insurance companies were formed to collect premiums and administer benefits. People began buying larger amounts of insurance in order to provide their families with coverage for contingencies other than burial expenses. Eventually, the concept of replacing income lost by a wage earner's unexpected death began to account for an increasing share of life insurance sales.

Today people count on life insurance for a wide variety of needs—providing for children's support and education, ensuring a life income for the surviving spouse and settling various debts, such as a mortgage or automobile loan. In addition, certain types of life insurance that accumulate cash values can be an important source of income when an insured wage earner lives on into the retirement period.[1]

However one chooses to plan for financial needs, the basic purpose of life insurance is to help solve a financial problem when a family's wage earner fails to "live long enough." Life insurance can therefore be contrasted with an annuity, which addresses the problem of "living too long" and thus exhausting one's savings.

CONSUMER ACCEPTANCE OF LIFE INSURANCE

The purchase of life insurance has long ranked high among the American consumer's financial objectives. By the end of 1985, the amount of life insurance in force for American families totaled over $6 trillion—an average of almost $75,000 per insured family. About 53% of this coverage was purchased by individuals, with the balance in various types of group insurance plans. The number of individual policies in force is about one and one-half times that of 25 years ago, and the average policy size has increased sixfold. Of this coverage, whole life policies represent the largest percentage by far—over 80% as compared to term insurance purchases.[2]

Why this great increase in the American public's purchase of life insurance? Many people buy life insurance because they view it as a way to protect their families' financial health. Also, life insurance companies traditionally have been quite aggressive in their marketing practices. By employing large sales forces and keeping their products competitive, they have made the public insurance conscious. Finally, new types of life insurance have also attracted many buyers.

Many recently introduced insurance products are marketed as savings and investment vehicles as much as they are for the death benefits they provide. In the past, many buyers used their life insurance to save money, even though the interest rates it paid were not competitive with those available from other savings products. However, interest earnings on insurance products have long enjoyed a tax-deferred status. (More details on income taxes and insurance will be provided later in this chapter.) In recent years, life insurance companies have begun to restructure their products to make them even more attractive to savers.[3]

BASIC TYPES OF LIFE INSURANCE POLICIES

While many types of life insurance policies are on the market, most can usually be classified as one of two types. The first—and original—type, known today as term insurance, provides only death protection. The second kind, permanent or whole life insurance, also incorporates a savings element. Both types pay a stated benefit to a survivor, known as the *beneficiary*, when the insured person dies.

Term Insurance

Term insurance is "pure" death protection; that is, it contains no savings element. As the name implies, term insurance covers a certain time period specified in the policy. This period can range from one to several years or even for life.[4]

Yearly renewable term is a widely sold policy form. It allows the insured to renew the policy each year without providing evidence of insurability, such as a physical examination that may have been required for the original issue. The premium for yearly renewable term goes up each year, because the cost of insurance rises. Life insurance companies use a mortality table such as the one in Figure 5-1 in establishing their rates. Such tables usually forecast how many people out of a group of 1,000 will die at a given age. For example, Figure 5-1 indicates that in a group of males age 21 there will be 1.91 deaths per 1,000. However, at age 50 that figure will rise to 6.71. The insurance company knows that it will be obligated to pay out more money insuring a 50-year-old male than it would a 21-year-old. Therefore, it will charge a 50-year-old applicant more than a younger one because of the likelihood of that person dying sooner. Other factors that insurance companies use in calculating their rates include administration, sales and other expenses.

Many insurance purchasers dislike the idea that their premiums increase each year. For this

FIGURE 5-1
Male Mortality Table*

Age	Deaths per 1,000	Expectation of Life (years)	Age	Deaths per 1,000	Expectation of Life (years)
0	4.18	70.83	51	7.30	24.52
1	1.07	70.13	52	7.96	23.70
2	.99	69.20	53	8.71	22.89
3	.98	68.27	54	9.56	22.08
4	.95	67.34	55	10.47	21.29
5	.90	68.40	56	11.46	20.51
6	.86	65.46	57	12.49	19.74
7	.80	64.52	58	13.59	18.99
8	.76	63.57	59	14.77	18.24
9	.74	62.62	60	16.08	17.51
10	.73	61.66	61	17.54	16.79
11	.77	60.71	62	19.19	16.08
12	.85	59.75	63	21.06	15.36
13	.99	58.80	64	23.14	14.70
14	1.15	57.86	65	25.42	14.04
15	1.33	56.93	66	27.85	13.39
16	1.51	56.00	67	30.44	12.76
17	1.67	55.09	68	33.19	12.14
18	1.78	54.18	69	36.17	11.54
19	1.86	53.27	70	39.51	10.96
20	1.90	52.37	71	43.30	10.39
21	1.91	51.47	72	47.65	9.84
22	1.89	50.57	73	52.64	9.30
23	1.86	49.66	74	58.19	8.79
24	1.82	48.75	75	64.19	8.31
25	1.77	47.84	76	70.53	7.84
26	1.73	46.93	77	77.12	7.40
27	1.71	46.01	78	83.90	6.97
28	1.70	45.09	79	91.05	6.57
29	1.71	44.16	80	98.84	6.18
30	1.73	43.24	81	107.48	5.80
31	1.78	42.31	82	117.25	5.44
32	1.83	41.38	83	128.26	5.09
33	1.91	40.46	84	140.25	4.77
34	2.00	39.54	85	152.95	4.46
35	2.11	38.61	86	166.09	4.18
36	2.24	37.69	87	179.55	3.91
37	2.40	36.78	88	193.27	3.66
38	2.58	35.87	89	207.29	3.41
39	2.79	34.96	90	221.77	3.18
40	3.02	34.05	91	236.98	2.94
41	3.29	33.16	92	253.45	2.70
42	3.56	32.26	93	272.11	2.44
43	3.87	31.38	94	295.90	2.17
44	4.19	30.50	95	384.55	1.54
45	4.55	29.62	96	329.96	1.87
46	4.92	28.76	97	480.20	1.20
47	5.32	27.90	08	657.98	.84
48	5.74	27.04	99	1,000.00	.50
49	6.21	26.20	100		
50	6.71	25.36			

*1980 Standard

Source: American Council of Life Insurance, Washington, D.C., 1987.

reason, companies have developed term plans with level premiums from year to year. Policies such as five-year term, ten-year term, term to age 65 and many others can be found in the marketplace. However, these are usually variations of yearly renewable term and are based on higher premiums than actually necessary in the early years, in order to maintain a level premium in later ones.

Permanent Insurance

Permanent or *whole life insurance* incorporates a savings element as well as death protection. Part of the purchaser's premium payments goes toward building a savings fund, known as the policy's *cash value.*

Like some forms of term insurance, many permanent plans have a level premium that generally does not go up in later years. Permanent insurance also incorporates a premium overcharge in order to maintain the coverage in later years, when mortality costs are higher. Unlike term insurance, however, with permanent insurance part of this overcharge and the subsequent interest earned accrues to the policyholder's account. This method builds the cash value in the policy. Some whole life policies pay annual dividends that increase the total cash value. The premium overcharge mentioned above contributes to the amount of the policy dividend. (More information on dividends is presented later in the chapter.)

The cash value of a whole life policy serves a variety of purposes. It can be used for collateral for an insurance company loan. If the insured decides to terminate the policy, he or she can elect to receive the policy's cash value at that time.

SPECIAL TYPES OF LIFE INSURANCE POLICIES

MODIFIED LIFE POLICY

Also known as a Graded Premium Whole Life, this plan features lower premiums in the early years and higher premiums later on.

For example, compare the premiums on a regular policy and a Graded Premium Whole Life Policy for $50,000 in insurance for a male, age 20:

Regular policy, annual premium
$662.50

Graded Premium Whole Life Policy
335.00   1st year (increasing through 4th year)

699.00   5th year and thereafter

JOINT LIFE POLICY

This policy covers the lives of two or more persons, and it is generally written on married couples or business partners. The benefit is paid on the person who dies first. It is less expensive than two individual policies, but is canceled upon the first death.

FAMILY PLAN POLICY

A combination of whole life and term insurance that provides insurance on all family members. This plan is usually sold in units; a typical unit provides $5,000 whole life on the head of the household, $1,250 on the spouse, and $1,000 on each child.

JUMPING JUVENILE POLICY

The policy is usually issued between birth to age 14 or 15. When the insured reaches age 21, face amount "jumps" to five times the original value with no increase in premium. For example, if a policy for $1,000 is issued on Jean at birth, at age 21 the face amount will automatically increase to $5,000 and the premium will remain the same.

(Additional benefits incorporated into permanent policies are covered later in the chapter.)

CONTRACT LAW BASIS OF LIFE INSURANCE

While life insurance is an accepted part of the average person's everyday financial affairs, many people may not consider its legal ramifications.

A life insurance policy is a legal contract that creates a relationship between two or more parties. The contract owner and the insurance company are the main parties, but others are involved. For example, the insured may be someone other than the contract owner. Then there are one or more beneficiaries—the individuals who are designated to receive the policy proceeds in the event of the insured's death.

Elements of Standard Contracts

It might be helpful at this point to delineate the essential elements of a contract. To be enforceable as a legally binding contract, the following six elements must be present:

1. an offer by one party and acceptance of the offer by another;
2. mutual consideration—that is, each party must give something and receive something;
3. competency of all parties to engage in the contract—namely, all parties must be legally capable of fulfilling their commitments in the contract;
4. a legal purpose;
5. true consent—that is, a "meeting of the minds" of all parties (For example, a contract would be unenforceable if one party signed because of threats or abuse.);
6. correct legal form.

Special Aspects of Life Insurance Contracts

While a life insurance policy falls within the accepted definition of a contract, it differs from many standard contracts in that it is unilateral, conditional, valued, adhesive and aleatory.

Unilateral

In a customary form of contract, each party agrees to perform in consideration for the promises of the others. A life insurance contract, however, is *unilateral* in that only one party's promise is legally enforceable: the insurance company's promise to pay death benefits if the insured dies while the policy is in effect. Once the initial premium has been paid and the policy is in force, the contract owner cannot be compelled to continue paying premiums and may not be held liable for breach of contract. The insurance company cannot completely void the contract if premiums are not paid, since certain continuing benefits may remain in effect even after the policy has lapsed (see the section "Nonforfeiture Options").

Life insurance contracts contain the possibly unique provision that even misrepresentation or concealment will not necessarily void the policy benefits. After a certain specified period, usually after two years, the insurance company cannot use these defenses against a claim even if the misstatements are later discovered and proven.[5]

Conditional

The insurance company's obligations can be described as *conditional*—enforceable only when the insured party or contract owner continues paying premiums and when the beneficiary furnishes the necessary proof of death (or disability, if the policy provides such a benefit). The company must then verify that the claim is legitimate and that the loss is covered under the policy terms.

Valued

A typical life insurance policy is *valued*—that is, it sets a face amount to be paid to the beneficiary in the event of the insured's death. In contrast, a property insurance contract might maintain that the insured item has depreciated over the years. For example, suppose that someone buys a fur coat and insures it for the purchase price of $10,000. Several years later, the coat is stolen and never recovered. Depending on the contract, the insurance company could pay only the coat's depreciated value, justifying this decision by claiming that even normal wear and tear on the coat has lessened its value. But a life insurance policy is considered a valued contract, and the entire specified amount must be paid to the beneficiary.

Adhesive

A contract of *adhesion* means that one party sets forth all the stipulations and the other either accepts all of them unconditionally or rejects the entire contract. In a life insurance contract, the insurance company sets forth the contract stipulations and the insured either accepts them without modification or declines the policy. The contract can be altered by endorsement or various other means, but the company drafts these modifications. To protect the insured's interests the courts have ruled that any dispute over a contract containing unclear language or other ambiguities will be resolved against the company.

Aleatory

The word *aleatory* refers to an occurrence dependent on chance. In an aleatory contract, one party may gain more than the other. Term insurance provides a good example of aleatory provisions. In a term contract, an insured person may pay one monthly premium of $25 and die, but the insurance company would have to pay out the entire face amount of the policy. The face amount might be $5,000, $50,000 or another sum. On the other hand, the insured may buy a 10-year term policy and pay premiums for 10 years for a total of, say, $5,000. If the insured survives the term the insurance company will have collected $5,000 but will not be obligated to pay out any.

LIFE INSURANCE POLICY CLAUSES

Life insurance contracts are subject to state regulations. While certain requirements differ from state to state, most states have adopted a standard policy provisions law and contract clauses tend to be fairly similar in provisions and wording. Among the major clauses common to most contracts are the ownership clause, entire contract clause, incontestable clause, suicide clause, grace period and reinstatement clause.

Ownership Clause

The *ownership clause* identifies the policy's owner. The owner can be the insured person, the beneficiary, or some other party; in most instances, the insured and the owner are the same. The ownership clause specifies that the policy owner has possession of the policy's contractual rights while the insured is alive. These rights generally include naming and changing beneficiaries, receiving dividends and accessing the policy's cash value.

Entire Contract Clause

The *entire contract clause* states that the life insurance policy and the application the insured person completes represent the complete contract between the parties. The insured's statements as recorded in the application are considered to be representations and not warranties or guarantees. The insured is not required to guarantee the validity of his or her statements on the application. Barring any unusual circumstances, this clause in effect confirms that the insured is only required to believe that the facts stated at the time of the application are correct.

The entire contract clause can provide some important protection for the policyholder. For example, the insured may be unaware of a current heart problem and make no mention of it on the application. Should death occur from this condition, the insurance company cannot necessarily deny any claims on the grounds that the applicant misrepresented material health information.

Incontestable Clause

The *incontestable clause* designates a period of time after which the insurance company cannot contest a claim because of misinformation on the original policy application. This period generally is one to two years from the date of the original application. Once the incontestable period expires, the company cannot deny a claim even if it discovers evidence of fraud or material misrepresentation. However, there are some exceptions to this rule. For example, if the company can prove that the beneficiary took out a policy with the intention of murdering the insured, it can contest the claim even after the incontestable period has expired.

Suppose that Robert, age 37, applies for insurance and conceals his blood pressure problem. He dies from this condition before the incontestable period expires. The insurance company's investigation ascertains that Robert was aware of his health problem and would be within its rights if it refused to pay the death benefit. However, what if Robert died after the incontestable period had expired? In that case, the company probably would have to pay the claim, other facts being equal, because the incontestable clause would preclude misrepresentation as a defense.

Suicide Clause

Most life insurance contracts typically contain a one- or two-year *suicide clause*. This clause provides that if the insured commits suicide within the specified time period, the policy will be considered void. In this case, only the amount of premiums paid in will be paid to the beneficiary. However, if the suicide occurs after the exclusion period, the regular death benefit will be paid. The purpose of this clause is to protect the insurance company against the case of an individual who takes out a policy with the intention of committing suicide shortly thereafter. When a claim is made, the insurance company bears the burden of proof to determine whether or not suicide was involved.

Grace Period

Most life insurance policies provide for a *grace period* for overdue premium payments. The company will keep the policy benefits in force for a limited time period even if the policyholder has not paid the regular premium. The grace period is usually limited to one month.

The object of this clause is to give the policy owner an extended period of time in which to pay the premium before the coverage lapses. When a premium payment is late, the insurance company customarily sends the insured a final notice warning that the grace period is about to expire. If the policy lapses, the owner may lose benefits unless he or she takes steps to reinstate it.

Reinstatement Clause

The *reinstatement clause* gives the policy owner the opportunity to reinstate a lapsed policy. By taking advantage of this clause, the insured may restore the benefits of the original contract and thus not have to apply for a new one. The insurance company typically makes some stipulations for reinstatement, such as requiring the insured to:

1. provide evidence of good health;
2. pay all overdue premiums;
3. repay any policy loans;
4. complete reinstatement requirements within a specified time period.

Reinstating a lapsed policy may have some advantages over applying for a new one. The premium on a new policy will probably be greater than that on the original since life insurance costs more as one ages. Also, by reinstating the original policy the insured need not qualify for a new incontestable period (see the section "Incontestable Clause").

BENEFICIARY DESIGNATIONS

The beneficiary designation names the person or persons who will receive the policy proceeds upon the insured's death. When proceeds become payable at this time, the insurance company in effect serves as a trustee of the funds. It makes the disbursements according to the insured's stipulations in the policy application or any later, superseding provisions.

Most insurance companies offer a variety of beneficiary designations. These can be arranged to suit most situations except complex trust arrangements, which might be better accomplished with a will. However, since life insurance proceeds pass directly to survivors rather than going through probate, it pays to explore the advantages of each beneficiary designation.

Insurance companies use certain terms in classifying beneficiaries. Among these are primary and contingent beneficiaries, revocable and irrevocable beneficiaries, and specific and class beneficiaries.

Primary and Contingent Beneficiaries

The *primary beneficiary* is the person who is first in line to receive proceeds upon the insured's death. For example, in a family situation, one spouse often names the other as primary beneficiary. The *contingent beneficiary* receives the policy benefits if the primary beneficiary is not living. For example, "children of the insured" might be listed as contingent beneficiaries. In this case, if the primary beneficiary—say, the wife—is not alive when death proceeds are payable, the children receive the policy benefits.

There may be complications if minor children are involved in the payment of benefits. Generally, insurance companies will not pay policy proceeds to underage children. Instead, an appointed guardian may receive payment to be held for the child. One solution is to have such a guardian appointed in a will; otherwise, a court may appoint the guardian, a process that often involves delays and legal expenses. An alternate solution is to designate the trust department of a bank to receive the proceeds. The bank trustee then disburses payments for the minor child as needed.

Some individuals name the insured's estate as primary or contingent beneficiary. Most financial planners advise against this course, however, since payment of proceeds may be delayed until the estate is settled and costs of probate may be involved.

Revocable and Irrevocable Beneficiaries

The standard *revocable beneficiary* designation gives the policy owner the right to revoke the beneficiary's status at any time. It is not required that the beneficiary consent to any changes or even be notified when this occurs. The revocable beneficiary, therefore, has only an expectation, not a guarantee, of benefits.

In contrast, the designation of *irrevocable beneficiary*, once made, can be changed only with the beneficiary's consent. For example, when an individual purchases life insurance in order to secure a loan, it is in the lender's interests to be named as the irrevocable beneficiary. Then, in the event of the insured/borrower's death, the lender will receive the proceeds.

Specific and Class Beneficiaries

Under a *specific beneficiary* designation, the beneficiary is specifically named and indicated. In contrast, a *class designation,* such as "children of the insured," is often used when the policy owner wishes to divide proceeds equally among a certain number of individuals. This designation occasionally leads to problems, and thus many companies restrict class designations. For instance, if children of a second marriage are involved, their inclusion as beneficiaries may be open to question.

OTHER IMPORTANT POLICY PROVISIONS

Life insurance contracts contain many other advantageous policy provisions. Among these are nonforfeiture options and settlement options.

Nonforfeiture Options

Policies that build cash values offer policyholders certain guarantees. Most insurance contracts cover long time periods, often of many years duration. Thus there is a possibility that at some point, for one reason or another, a policy owner will discontinue payment and allow the policy to lapse. Should this occur, certain guarantees in the policy will come into operation. These guarantees are designated as *nonforfeiture options.* As the term implies, they refer to safeguards for the policy owner that the insurance company cannot abridge.[6]

Most states have adopted nonforfeiture regulations that specify minimum provisions for the protection of policy owners who decide to discontinue their policies. These provisions are cash value and residual policy benefits, including reduced paid-up insurance and extended term insurance.

Cash Value

A policy may be surrendered at any time for its listed cash value. The cash value is customarily indicated on a yearly basis in the policy and increases by the amount of any dividends not previously paid out to the policyholder. In the early years of a policy, little actual cash value accumulates because the company must pay substantial acquisition costs in putting the policy in force. These costs cover the insurance salesperson's commissions, the investigation of the applicant, the evaluation of health and financial information, and various other administrative functions. In later years, however, substantial cash values can build.

Residual Policy Benefits

There are two important policy benefits typically offered to policyholders who choose to stop paying premiums: reduced paid-up insurance and extended term insurance. Either of these options allows the policyholder to leave the cash value on deposit with the insurance company instead of canceling the policy for cash.

The *reduced paid-up insurance* option keeps a designated amount of paid-up life insurance in force even if no further premium payments are made. This amount is specified in the policy.

This benefit is provided regardless of the age at which the insured dies. For example, look at Figure 5-2. Suppose the insured stops paying premiums in the tenth policy year. If the original face

FIGURE 5-2
Nonforfeiture Options*

End of policy year	Cash or loan value	Paid-up insurance	Extended Term Insurance	
			Years	Days
1	$ 0.00	$ 0	0	0
2	0.00	0	0	0
3	4.79	15	1	315
4	16.21	48	6	161
5	27.91	81	11	15
6	39.91	113	14	275
7	52.20	145	17	158
8	64.78	176	19	157
9	77.66	206	20	342
10	90.84	236	22	29
11	104.33	265	22	351
12	118.13	294	23	231
13	132.25	322	24	54
14	146.69	350	24	191
15	161.43	377	24	290
16	176.47	403	24	356
17	191.79	429	25	28
18	207.38	454	25	42
19	223.22	478	25	36
20	239.29	502	25	13
Age 60	563.42	806	17	26
Age 65	608.49	833	15	272

* Dollar amount for each $1,000 of face amount of insurance

Source: *Principles of Insurance*, George Rejda, (Scott, Foresman and Company, 1986). Reprinted by permission

amount of the policy was $100,000, the reduced paid-up amount will be $23,600. No matter how long the insured lives, $23,600 will be paid as a death benefit upon his or her decease.

With the extended term insurance option, the full original face amount of the policy remains in force for a limited time period after premium payments are discontinued. Again referring to Figure 5-2, suppose the policy owner stops paying premiums in year 10. Term insurance protection for the full original face amount, $100,000, will stay in effect for a period of 22 years and 29 days. At the end of that time, the policy will lapse with no cash value.

Settlement Options

Like annuities, life insurance policies feature a wide choice of settlement options (see Chapter 2). One additional option that pertains only to life insurance proceeds is known as the *interest only option*. Here the company holds the death proceeds and pays out only interest, usually at intervals requested by the beneficiary. The policy typically specifies a guaranteed minimum interest rate; however, the effective rate (the rate actually paid) may be increased according to the company's earnings.

Settlement options offer some convenience and safety in that the insurance company provides principal and interest guarantees and hence an assured income for the insured's survivors. However, economic conditions at the time of the insured's death may dictate alternate choices. There may be other equally safe and convenient investments that offer more competitive interest rates.

Another point to consider is the lack of flexibility of settlement options. Many companies prohibit beneficiaries from changing methods of withdrawal once they have chosen a settlement option. Practically speaking, this means that even if emergency financial needs arise, a beneficiary may receive no lump sum distributions once he or she has chosen a settlement option. There are more flexible methods of investing insurance proceeds than leaving them on deposit with the company.

LIFE INSURANCE DIVIDENDS

Life insurance dividends actually represent a partial refund of money paid as premiums. As pointed out earlier in the chapter, a life insurance dividend results mainly from an overcharge on the premium. This overcharge is imposed to keep the premium level during the contract's life. Other factors involved in dividend calculations are based on a combination of mortality experience, administrative cost savings and interest returns.

To understand the composition of a life insurance dividend, consider how the insurance company calculates the cost of providing a death benefit. Each year that an individual lives, the cost of insurance goes up, since the likelihood of death increases. The typical whole life insurance contract is constructed so that in the early years, when the cost of insurance is lower, the premium contains an overcharge. Both the overcharge and the corresponding interest earnings help build up the policy's cash value. This increased total cash value, in turn, enables the insurance company to provide coverage for a level amount of premium dollars in later years when the cost of insurance normally is relatively expensive.

Since predictions of mortality and interest earnings cannot be exact, favorable outcomes in these areas result in a dividend. In essence then, the dividend is a refund of the overcharge made in estimating future results. Most insurance companies provide prospective purchasers with estimates of future dividends. These estimates normally are accompanied by a statement to the effect that dividend figures are not guaranteed but are forecasted based on past experience. Actual dividends paid may, of course, vary from these projections. It is possible that for certain years dividends will be omitted entirely. This is unlikely, however, because insurance companies are usually conservative in estimating future dividends.[7]

METHODS OF DIVIDEND PAYMENT

Dividends usually become payable during the second or third year of a policy's life. Dividends may be paid in any of the following ways.

- **Cash Payment** If the policy owner chooses cash payment, he or she usually receives a check for the amount of the dividend on the policy's anniversary.
- **Accumulation of Interest** Dividends may be left on deposit with the insurance company, in which case they will earn interest. Often there is a basic guaranteed rate, but the actual rate credited is usually higher. The effective rate is based on current economic conditions but is often below that of banks, savings and loan associations and other financial

institutions. Most companies permit withdrawal of dividend accumulations at the policyholder's option. If left on deposit, these accumulations will be added to the cash value when the policy matures or is surrendered. If the insured dies, the dividends will be paid in addition to the policy's face amount.

- **Application to Reduce Premiums**   The policyholder may choose to use the annual dividend to reduce the regular premium payment. In that case, the insurance company automatically applies the amount of the dividend to reduce the premium and bills the policyholder for the net amount due.

- **Paid-Up Additions**   Dividends may be used to purchase additional amounts of insurance that are considered paid up. For example, suppose a 21-year old male owns a policy with a $10,000 face amount and receives a dividend of $50. He could elect to apply the dividend toward the purchase of additional life insurance. For a person of his age, the amount purchased could constitute about $200 in additional death benefits, which would be added to the basic $10,000 if he died. No further payment would be needed to keep the $200 addition in force, although, of course, the regular annual premium would have to be paid in order to maintain the base policy.[8]

SINGLE-PREMIUM WHOLE LIFE

The array of life insurance products offered to the public today is almost bewildering. Many traditional varieties of both term and permanent insurance are available, and new types are constantly appearing. It is beyond the scope of this book to describe even a select few of these in detail. This section, therefore, describes one of the most widely marketed policy forms—the single-premium whole life policy.

Advantages of Single-Premium Whole Life

The *single-premium whole life policy* is basically a whole life insurance plan that is purchased with a single payment.[9] Most people are more familiar with the traditional kind of policy that is purchased with a series of payments made at specified intervals. However, single-premium life has become quite popular in recent years and is now being marketed by many savings institutions that offer tax-deferred annuity plans. Its major attractions are generous death benefits and tax-free distributions of interest earnings through loan provisions.

Death Benefits
The single-premium life contract offers a substantial death benefit. For example, a contract with a $10,000 premium might provide the following coverage:

Age at Policy Issue	Death Benefit Male	Female
21	$106,570	132,030[10]
30	71,910	88,250
45	37,630	46,480
55	26,180	31,980

Simply stated, the above table indicates that a male purchaser, age 21, who paid a premium of $10,000 would be insured for the sum of $106,570 in addition to other benefits stipulated in the policy. A 45-year-old female purchaser would be covered for $46,480, the difference being due, of course, to her greater age.

Tax-Advantaged Interest Earnings

The interest earnings of single-premium whole life policies offer some considerable tax advantages. Earnings accumulate with no current income tax consequences, and under current tax law, distributions of interest may be made free of income taxes by using policy loan provisions. Further, interest rates on single-premium life policies have been quite competitive with CD rates in recent years.

In addition to the above-listed death benefit feature, the single-premium contract provides earnings on the money paid to the insurance company. In the single-premium policy described above, assume interest is paid on the $10,000 at an 8% rate guaranteed for one year. At the end of the year, the funds will have earned the 8% and the policy's cash value will be credited with $800. With many policies of this type, there is no additional charge for the death benefit.

Interest rates are often set on an annual basis, although some have shorter guarantee periods. Some contracts also guarantee a minimum rate for the life of the contract.

Owners of single-premium life plans enjoy another major advantage: by taking advantage of their contracts' policy loan provisions, they can withdraw earnings from their policies and not be subject to income taxes. The Internal Revenue Code currently provides that loans made to the owner of a life insurance policy are not considered taxable income. One can obtain a series of loans from a company with no formal repayment schedule. When the insured dies, the total amount of the loans is subtracted from the face amount of the policy's death benefit and the balance passes to the beneficiary. This is also a tax-free disbursement, since life insurance death benefits normally are not subject to income taxes.

Types of Single-Premium Plans

Like annuities, single-premium life plans are offered with both fixed and variable investment portfolios. One current fixed plan offers a rate comparable to that for a long-term CD. The initial rate is guaranteed for three policy years. In subsequent periods, the contract pays interest comparable to that for 91-day Treasury bills; however, the plan guarantees a minimum rate of a few points below the initial interest rate.

Some companies offer single-premium variable policies that include many of the features of the variable annuities described in Chapter 4. Like variable annuity plans, these variable policies are based on some form of equity investment and typically offer several types of mutual funds, money market accounts and government securities along with guaranteed fixed accounts.

Uses of Single-Premium Plans

One suitable use for a single-premium policy is for retirement purposes. A couple approaching retirement can invest a lump sum into the plan and then borrow from it on an annual basis to produce tax-free income. As stated earlier, at the insured's death the insurance company subtracts the outstanding amount of the loan from the death benefit and pays the surviving party the balance. This lump sum payment is also tax-free.

Another useful application concerns a child's educational fund. A parent can set up an educational investment fund by purchasing a single-premium life policy. The fund earns interest free of current taxes. When the child reaches college age, the parent can borrow money from the policy, again on a tax-free basis. This arrangement provides the additional advantage of life insurance in the event of the family head's death during this period. Such an arrangement in effect supplants more complex trust agreements in which funds are set aside in the child's name for tax purposes. The tax benefits of these types of trusts generally have been curtailed by recent tax reform legislation. The single-premium plan offers a simple, convenient plan for an educational fund that grows on a tax-deferred basis and remains under the parent's complete control.

A single-premium life plan can also be used to set up custodial funds for an elderly parent. For example, a son can purchase a single-premium policy and use annual loans to generate a tax-free maintenance fund for a parent or grandparent. If the son dies, the death benefit will create additional custodial funds.

Some financial planners have found further uses for single-premium life in meeting various family needs. Figure 5-3 illustrates how one family might set aside funds in such a program to achieve different objectives.

Using this example, suppose that Peter Andrews, age 35, has $100,000 to invest. His family needs no additional current income at this time. Peter wants to invest the money without having to pay current income taxes on the interest earnings. Peter's first priority for this investment is to ensure adequate educational funds for his son,

FIGURE 5-3
Meeting Various Family Needs Through Single Premium Life*

End of Policy Year	Annual Loan	Loan Balance	Value Accumulation	Net Cash Surrender Value	Net Death Benefit	
1	$ 0	$ 0	$5107,500	$100,000	$462,952	
2	0	0	115,562	106,318	462,952	
3	0	0	124,229	115,534	462,952	Initial life
4	0	0	133,546	125,534	462,952	insurance
5	0	0	143,562	136,385	462,952	protection
6	0	0	154,330	148,157	462,952	
7	0	0	165,904	160,928	462,952	
8	0	0	178,347	174,781	462,952	
9	0	0	191,723	189,807	462,952	
10	0	0	206,103	206,103	462,952	
11	10,000	10,000	221,560	211,561	466,355	
12	10,000	20,800	238,227	217,428	477,096	
13	10,000	32,464	256,199	223,735	487,620	
14	20,000	55,061	275,576	220,515	487,824	
15	10,000	69,466	296,519	227,054	496,886	
16	10,000	85,023	319,106	234,083	505,323	
17	10,000	101,825	343,464	241,639	509,541	
18	0	109,971	369,733	259,762	522,272	
19	0	118,768	398,013	279,244	533,972	
20	0	128,270	428,457	300,187	544,408	
21	30,000	168,531	461,233	292,702	523,318	
22	0	182,014	496,668	314,654	543,121	
23	0	196,575	534,828	338,253	562,881	
24	30,000	242,301	575,923	333,622	552,473	
25	0	261,685	620,329	358,644	569,555	
26	0	282,620	668,162	385,542	585,991	
27	0	305,230	719,688	414,458	615,970	
28	0	329,648	775,191	445,542	647,091	
29	0	356,020	834,978	478,958	679,352	
(Age 65) 30	35,922	420,424	899,882	478,958	676,821	

Tax-free retirement income that doesn't reduce Social Security

Downpayments for son's and daughter's homes

Son's tuition

Daughter's tuition

Life insurance protection at age 65

*Projected Values Illustrating End-of-Year Loan Option
(based on 7.5% assumed interest for illustration purposes only)

Source: Financial Planning Uses of Single Premium Life Insurance,
Jackson National Life Insurance Company, Lansing, MI, 1987.

who is presently 8 years old, and daughter, now age 4.

Assuming an interest rate of 7½%, in 10 years the original $100,000 has more than doubled. In the 11th year, when Peter's son is 18, Peter makes withdrawals of $10,000 each year for four years, in the form of tax-free policy loans. In year 14, he takes out a $20,000 policy loan because his daughter is now college age ($10,000 of this represents the last year of the son's college tuition). From years 15 through 17, Peter borrows $10,000 each year to complete the daughter's education. Although $80,000 has been withdrawn in the form of policy loans, the policy's net cash surrender value at this time would be $241,639.

Four years later, Peter gives his son $30,000 for a downpayment on a home and does the same for his daughter three years after that. Peter makes no further withdrawals from the policy until he reaches age 65, at which time he may begin drawing a retirement income of up to $35,922 without depleting any principal. Again, because of the borrowing arrangement, this money is free of income taxes and does not reduce Social Security benefits as other income might. Also, at this point the principal remaining in the policy is enough to supply a tax-free death benefit of $676,821— several times higher than Peter's original $100,000 premium.

The above example graphically illustrates how the purchase of a single-premium whole life policy can lend itself to a financial planning situation. One initial investment has served many purposes over several years and has permitted both a tax-free accumulation and tax-free withdrawals of interest earnings.

Investor Considerations

Single-premium life policies obviously offer many advantages to the individual consumer as a financial planning tool. However, they also entail some special considerations.

Investment Risk

There may be some investment risk in single-premium life purchases. Like annuities, funds in life insurance policies are not covered by federal deposit insurance; they are backed by the issuing company. However, most states require that insurance companies contribute to a special fund that will safeguard policyholders' rights within the contract, including cash values and death benefits. The provisions of this fund become operable in case of an insurance company's insolvency. However, a prospective purchaser of such plans should assume the responsibility for investigating the company to determine the soundness of the investment. The savings institution offering the product should be able to supply adequate background information on the issuer's financial status and history. The customer may also consult *Best's Insurance Reports,* a standard insurance rating guide, as well as other consumer publications.

Liquidity of Funds

Another consideration in purchasing a single-premium life insurance contract is the liquidity, or availability, of one's funds. As described earlier, policy loans are a convenient way to make tax-free withdrawals from a single-premium plan. However, if the contract owner wants to cash in the policy, there may be some liquidity problems. If the policy's total value is redeemed from the insurance company, all profits earned will become taxable at that time, and the income tax payable can be substantial.

Another problem might arise after a series of policy loans. If the amount of policy loans begins to deplete the policy's basic cash value, there may be income tax consequences. However, as long as there is some minimum amount—specified by the insurance company—left in the contract to fund the death benefit to the beneficiary, coverage will not lapse and the IRS will not maintain that the policy has been surrendered for cash. This should preclude any income tax problems. The company normally notifies the policyholder of an impending policy lapse. At that point, the company might advise the policyholder to discontinue borrowing or to repay a loan.

Investment Charges

Single-premium life plans generally entail no sales fees per se, with the exception of plans with variable investment portfolios. The latter are subject to the same types of investment management fees incurred with variable annuity products (described in Chapter 4). However, there are usually surrender charges involved in early redemption of the contract. A typical single-premium life plan would incorporate a declining surrender charge for a period of six years. In that case there would be a charge of 6% of the total amount invested if the policy were cashed in during the first year, 5% for the second year and so on, and none by the end of the sixth year. Obviously, the policy owner should take this into account unless he or she will not need the original principal amount for a number of years.

Policy loans may incur interest charges. However, many companies will credit the policy with the exact amount of interest charged. The net result in this case is that the customer will incur no interest on borrowed policy earnings. However, should the policyholder want to borrow on the principal amount, the company will probably charge a net interest rate. This situation is similar to taking a passbook or CD loan at a savings institution, where there is a charge for borrowing but regular interest continues to be paid on the account owner's funds.

In the section "Tax Advantaged Interest Earnings," a situation was illustrated in which the full amount of the promised interest rate is credited to the policy and there is no charge for the death benefit. However, this is not necessarily true of all single-premium life policies. Some companies advertise a stated interest rate but subtract the cost of providing the death benefit from policy earnings. The inevitable result of this practice is a net earnings rate that is lower than it originally appears.

MARKETING OF INSURANCE PLANS BY SAVINGS INSTITUTIONS

Many savings institutions that traditionally have offered tax-deferred annuity products are also marketing life insurance plans. While some institutions offer a wide variety of plans, many focus only on single-premium life products. One possible reason for this is the similarities of single-premium plans to the tax-deferred annuities already offered.

The public's increasing acceptance of single-premium life has been largely due to its growing importance as a tax-sheltered product. Tax rulings in recent years appear to have clarified its tax-deferred status. However, like IRAs, tax-deferred annuities and other products, the income tax status of single-premium life may be subject to change in the future.

FOOTNOTES

[1]Life insurance companies have developed detailed methods for calculating a family's insurance needs including provisions for dependent children, life income provisions for the surviving spouse, emergency funds and other factors.

[2]*Life Insurance Fact Book* (Washington, DC: American Council of Life Insurance, 1986).

[3]While life insurance is marketed as an investment product, some important distinctions set it apart from most other types of investments. One is qualification. Insurance companies do not automatically insure everyone who applies. Most require prospective purchasers to provide evidence of reasonably good health before they will issue policies. If a company discovers some health impairment, it may grant the insurance but charge an extra fee, known as a *rating*. Insurance companies also usually investigate an applicant's ability to pay. These health and financial requirements often are waived when offering life insurance to groups of individuals. Common examples of group insurance are employer plans and coverages for members of various types of associations.

[4]Term for life is often designated *term to age 100*.

[5]This provision prevents the insurance company from denying a claim unless there has been material misrepresentation on the applicant's part—and even then it may be unable to do so (see the section "Incontestable Clause"). For example, material misrepresentation might be charged if the applicant had concealed the existence of an incurable, life-threatening disease, as compared with a minor misrepresentation such as a few years misstatement of age.

[6]While nonforfeiture options generally apply only to policies that accumulate cash value, some term policies, particularly long-term ones, that have small cash values also contain nonforfeiture options.

[7]Dividends are paid on what is termed *participating policies*. Policies that do not provide for dividends are known as *nonparticipating policies*—that is, they do not participate in the company's annual divisible surplus. Nonparticipating policies often cost less initially than participating policies. They are also known as *net cost* contracts, because the purchaser knows in advance what the net cost will be. However, the overall cost of the participating policy might be substantially less, depending on the dividends paid.

[8]Some companies offer a *fifth dividend option*. With this option, an individual purchases a certain amount of one-year term insurance. The face amount of the insurance is determined by the amount of the dividend and the rates that the company charges.

[9]Some single-premium life plans provide for additional deposits at the policyholder's option.

[10]Mortality tables indicate that females live longer than males. The incidence of death risk is lower on females, and the insurance company can provide a larger amount of life insurance for the same premium amount.

6

RELATING PRODUCTS TO CUSTOMERS

- Understanding common barriers to financial planning

- Definition of consultative selling

- Qualities of the consultative sales-person

- Sales interview process

- Licensing requirements for the counselor

P RESENTING THE CONCEPTS of mutual funds, annuities and single-premium life insurance to customers can be a challenging task for the savings counselor. Communication problems may arise because of the complexity and unfamiliarity of these products. It is difficult for anyone to make a good buying decision when he or she does not understand the products that are available. In addition, the counselor must address the customer's concerns about retirement, educational planning for children, life expectancy, survivor's benefits and other weighty topics. The decision to invest in an annuity or life insurance often involves the consideration of one's values and life objectives. In effect, the purchase of the investment products presented in this book entails elements of personal financial planning.

While savings counselors are not financial planners, they can develop skills that will enhance their customers' ability to make sound financial decisions. This chapter focuses on these skills. Counselors can help customers overcome factors that commonly deter them from planning their finances and purchasing appropriate investment products with specific techniques. Counselors can help correlate investment products with customers' financial goals and objectives. The chapter also covers licensing requirements entailed in presenting these products to customers.

OVERCOMING COMMON BARRIERS

Counselors may hear these or similar statements from their customers:

- I keep meaning to start up one of those annuities, but I don't have the time.

- I won't be retiring for a long time. Besides, those thoughts depress me.
- Yes, it would be smart for me to diversify. But before I make a decision, I want to have a lot of information. Making good investment decisions is tricky.
- Frankly, I'd like to learn about that investment. But I get too uncomfortable talking with those aggressive salespeople. I don't want to be pressured.

These statements reflect some of the concerns that keep many individuals from benefiting from the new types of investment products that their savings institutions offer. They are common reactions.

Placing money in new types of investments represents a change for individuals who are accustomed to relying exclusively on deposit services. Individuals react differently in the way they respond to change. In many cases, people's resistance to change depends on the number and types of barriers that prevent them from acknowledging how the changes could benefit them. This section examines some common barriers to consumers' acceptance of new investment products and possible strategies for overcoming them.

"I Don't Have the Time."

Time is a limited resource for everyone. Counselors face two problems regarding time. First, the demands of careers and families leave most customers with little spare time. Second, many people believe that investing in unfamiliar products such as those discussed in this book is a time-consuming process. They may think that the process requires hours of reading complicated materials and completing forms. They may also believe that it would take too much time to meet with counselors personally and to have funds transferred from existing accounts into other investments.

Customers' unwillingness to spend time on personal financial matters presents two challenges for counselors. First, counselors must be able to convince customers that spending a reasonable amount of time selecting and applying for appropriate investment products is a smart thing to do. Second, they must help customers recognize that the purchase of a new investment need not be a time-consuming process.

Counselors can help customers recognize the benefits of devoting time to financial decision making by explaining the importance of financial planning. The best financial decisions are made when the decision-making process begins by defining the customer's goals and objectives. The counselor can explain the value of this process by emphasizing that the time needed for gathering information from the customer will be worthwhile, for example:

> Yes, I would be glad to give you information on annuities. Before I go too far into details, let me ask if you are considering an annuity as a long-term or short-term investment? Let's take a few minutes to review what you want to accomplish so you can see how this investment could work for you.

The counselor can also overcome real and perceived lack-of-time problems by emphasizing the ease with which an investment can be made:

- Opening an annuity is as easy as opening a certificate of deposit. You can apply today by completing this short application.

- If you have money in an account at another bank, we can arrange for it to be transferred here for you.
- The chart in this brochure gives you all of that information in one handy place.

The counselor can also communicate a sense of time efficiency by being organized and well-prepared for meetings with customers. All necessary forms, brochures and other materials should be in order on the counselor's desk so that the customer's time is not wasted. The counselor can also speed up the process by completing some parts of the transaction before or after a face-to-face or telephone meeting with the customer.

"Those Thoughts Depress Me."

Customers often are averse to contemplating drastic changes in their life situations. The subjects of death, retirement and estate distribution can be disturbing. For example, attorneys who regularly prepare wills for clients often hear their clients say, "*If* I die"; rarely does an individual say, "*When* I die." Still other people never get around to making out a will at all. In many cases, the real reason for this procrastination is a reluctance to deal with an unsettling element of reality. Death is not the only subject that many people are reluctant to discuss. Some people are uncomfortable in planning for their children's college education or for their retirement because they are anxious about growing old. The savings counselor must realize that these feelings may make it difficult for customers to make and implement good financial plans.

To see how this situation might arise during an interview, consider the case of a counselor presenting the merits of a single-premium life policy. After some discussion, the counselor recognizes that this product may be suitable for this customer's particular financial needs. The customer acknowledges that he could benefit from the income tax advantages, competitive interest rate and other features. However, when the counselor begins to explain the death provisions, the customer suddenly backs off. This sudden reluctance is surprising to the counselor; at first the product seemed to fulfill all of the customer's expressed needs. The customer was comfortable with the counselor's presentation until he was asked to consider a subject that made him uncomfortable—his death.

One way for the counselor to overcome this potential barrier to the sale is to highlight the product's more positive aspects. With single-premium life insurance, for example, the tax-free withdrawal provisions are good points to reiterate, as are the favorable interest returns and various policy guarantees. The counselor can play down the death benefit while centering the discussion around the advantages the customer will enjoy while still living.

In other situations in which the counselor recognizes that customers are uncomfortable discussing certain topics, the counselor can use the same strategy. For example, if a prospective annuity customer does not seem interested in discussing his or her retirement years, the counselor can focus on other benefits of owning an annuity.

"Making Good Investment Decisions Is Tricky."

Customers' hesitation in making buying decisions is often a symptom of a lack of confidence in their ability to make a good decision. Many people feel that they are not skilled in the processes that result in good decisions. Customers may also feel uncertain because they lack the proper information about a product or do not understand the information they have received. Also, they may have made a bad decision in the past and now wish to avoid any more potentially bad situations.

It is not surprising that many people feel unqualified to make good financial decisions. Decision making and problem solving are not included in the curricula in most high schools and colleges. Therefore most people do not have training in these skills. Most media advertising today encourages people to make purchase decisions based upon emotional responses rather than a rational process. Advertisements tend to concentrate on products and their features as an end in themselves. They do not encourage prospective buyers to identify their needs and to then find products that will enable them to satisfy those needs. As a result, people often find that they have purchased products that really do not match their needs.

Third, much of the vocabulary that is used in investments is unfamiliar to many people. The use of jargon creates communication problems. As a result, even those people who feel confident in their decision-making ability are sometimes intimidated by those who are selling investment products.

Counselors can help customers to overcome any lack of confidence in their ability to make careful decisions by guiding them through a logical decision-making process. Good financial decisions begin with an examination of the investor's goals and objectives. By helping the investor to discuss and set priorities for arriving at goals and objectives, the counselor helps to set the stage for a decision that is well founded. Next, the investor's present investment portfolio is studied. This step helps investors look at how their resources are currently employed and evaluate their investment strategies. Finally, new products are considered and selected. In this final step, the counselor is responsible for presenting product information in clear, accurate terms. This process is compared to another common decision-making process, product comparison, in Figure 6-1.

Using this procedure helps assure the customer that the decision has been reached through a rational process. It can also strengthen the relationships between the institution and the customer because it demonstrates that the institution places the customer's needs ahead of its sales goals. This process can be valuable to the customer and to the institution and it is the basis of the sales process that is presented later in this chapter.

"I Don't Want to Be Pressured."

Some people avoid talking with a counselor about financial products because they anticipate that the counselor's goal is to sell products rather than to

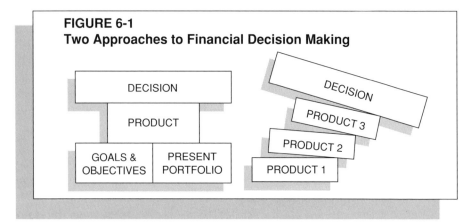

FIGURE 6-1
Two Approaches to Financial Decision Making

DECISION

PRODUCT

GOALS & OBJECTIVES | PRESENT PORTFOLIO

DECISION

PRODUCT 3

PRODUCT 2

PRODUCT 1

help customers satisfy their financial needs. Often, people feel intimidated by salespeople and find it difficult to refuse them or to end a conversation with a salesperson even if they have no interest in the product the salesperson is presenting. The perception of counselors as aggressive salespeople can prevent customers from taking advantage of the knowledge and service the counselor can offer.

Counselors can help customers recognize that they will not feel pressured into purchasing certain products by carefully following the sales process established by their institution. Savings institutions traditionally have employed a "soft-sell" type of selling method. In the *soft-sell process,* or *consultative selling,* discussed in the next section, the counselor helps the customer gather all of the information necessary for making a sound decision. This method contrasts with high-pressure sales, in which completion of the sale rather than the customer's needs is given top priority. The soft-sell method works for savings institutions because it reflects their trusting, long-term relationships with their customers.

CONSULTATIVE SELLING

Consultative selling can be considered both a sales process and a selling philosophy. Its successful implementation incorporates two important objectives:

1. to help the counselor project empathy for the customer's needs and objectives;

2. to create an environment of impartiality and

objectivity while presenting solutions for customer problems.

These objectives may seem difficult to achieve in a sales interview, but they are basic to acquiring a professional selling attitude. By using consultative selling techniques and converting them into a natural, comfortable presentation style, the counselor can avoid a "one-size-fits-all" approach to dealing with customers.

A consultative selling interview begins with eliciting information on the customer's preferences for handling personal finances. The counselor first asks the customer to express personal opinions on how economic factors such as inflation and taxes affect his or her investment plans. Once the counselor has this information, the discussion progresses to the customer's feelings on such matters as safety and liquidity of investments. Will he or she accept some element of risk in an investment if it offers the possibility of a higher return than would otherwise be available? Must savings and investments be as liquid as possible, or may at least some funds be set aside for longer periods?

Such discussions lead to further customer concerns, such as: Is growth of the investment more important than current income? Must investments be uncomplicated and fairly simple to manage? Will other family members easily understand the family portfolio and be able to take over in an emergency?

By showing an understanding of the customer's preferences, the counselor conveys a genuine interest in the customer's personal concerns. This type of interchange creates a truly professional consulting atmosphere. The customer will not be thinking, "This person is here merely to sell me something."

The savings counselor can avoid any suggestion of pressure in the sales interview by observing the line between giving information and dispensing investment advice when presenting investment solutions to customers. This is not always easy to do. However, two techniques can help counselors separate giving information from providing advice while still supplying adequate customer service. One method is to make extensive use of facts, with minimal opinions. The other is to employ neutral words and statements in the presentation, avoiding judgmental comments.

When providing facts for customers, the information should be based on reliable sources and be as current as possible. Furthermore, facts should be related such that they can be verified by outside sources that the customer might want to investigate. It is also appropriate for the counselor to cite opinions about products provided they are from reliable sources and identified as such. On the other hand, personal opinions on actions the customer should take will almost always appear to be advice; thus, it is wise to avoid such statements entirely.

By employing neutral words in a sales situation, the counselor can avoid projecting personal opinions. For example, suppose the customer is considering investing in municipal bonds but admits to being in a low tax bracket. The counselor should not say, "Well, in that case, you shouldn't go into municipal bonds; they'd be a bad investment for you." A more neutral statement would consist of stressing municipal bonds' generally low return relative to a comparable investment in, say, corporate bonds. With this particular customer, the tax advantage of municipal bonds would be negligible. Giving this information in nonjudgmental terms will help avoid the appearance of providing investment recommendations.

QUALITIES OF THE CONSULTATIVE SALESPERSON

Selling financial products that will enable customers to meet their objectives is a natural part of good customer service. While it is natural, it is not an inborn ability. The successful consultative salesperson must learn and practice a complex set of skills and attitudes. To succeed in consultative sales, a counselor needs to be:

1. knowledgeable about institution's products;
2. knowledgeable about common investment issues;
3. able to relate products to customer needs and objectives;
4. aware of responsibilities to both customer and institution.

Knowledgeable about Products

The counselor should be thoroughly familiar with the products offered by the savings institution. This is not a simple task considering the growing variety of products in today's marketplace. However, customers have a right to expect the institution's employees to know the details necessary to a buying decision. Undoubtedly there will be times when the counselor cannot immediately answer questions. Nevertheless, the counselor should know where to find the answers and see to it that the customer gets a reasonably prompt response. Customers are seldom offended when a counselor cannot provide an immediate response to every question. On the contrary, they are often impressed with an honest "I don't know," particularly if coupled with "But I'll do my best to find out for you," followed by prompt action. Handling customers in this manner helps reinforce the counselor's professional image.

Knowledgeable about Common Investment Issues

While each customer has a unique set of experiences and concerns, many investors share some common concerns. The impact of inflation and taxes on the value of investments is one of these common concerns. Balancing risks and return is also a consideration that arises frequently when customers consider investment options. The ability to discuss these common investment issues is an important quality for counselors.

Effect of Inflation and Taxes

Many people agree that inflation and income taxes are prime considerations when contemplating an investment. Of course, it is important to calculate how many dollars one can expect as an investment return. But to be practical, one must consider what those dollars might be worth in future purchasing power and how many dollars will go to income taxes.

There is a quick, convenient way to illustrate the effects of inflation and taxes. The counselor can easily calculate for the customer the rate of return needed just to break even over any period of years when incorporating the effects of inflation and income taxes. This point is demonstrated in the following example using 6% as the projected annual inflation rate and 28% as the customer's tax bracket. The number 6 is used as the numerator and 72 as the denominator, since 72 represents the figure remaining when 28, the income tax percentage, is subtracted from 100:

$$\frac{\text{Inflation Rate}}{100\%\text{-tax rate}} = \frac{6\%}{100\%\text{-}28\%} = \frac{6\%}{72\%} = 8.33\%$$

Thus, a customer in the 28% tax bracket must earn 8.33% on an investment in order to retain its purchase value under a 6% inflation rate. This same formula can be used for customers in other situations by changing the numbers. The numerator should always be the rate of inflation and the difference between the investor's tax rate and 100 should be the denominator.

This calculation dramatizes one of the problems that the average investor faces today and can be used later in the interview when discussing tax-advantaged investments.

Risk and Return
It is important for the counselor to know how much investment risk the customer will accept and what he or she needs in terms of ready availability of funds. If this concern surfaced earlier in the discussion, it can be helpful at this point to review and expand on it. If, for example, the customer has shown a decided preference for investments that offer guarantees of principal and interest, he or she may react aversely to a suggestion of mutual funds.

However, such a preference does not necessarily preclude discussing other methods of investing. For example, during a sales interview, the customer might come to an understanding of how taxes and inflation affect the value of an investment. With that knowledge, the customer may express an interest in earning a return that would

RULE OF 72

The rule of 72 is a well-known mathematical formula for a rule of thumb estimate of the effects of compound interest. The following are two examples of how this formula can be used.

Example:
Dividing the number 72 by the percentage of return that money is earning will indicate the number of years it will take to double an investment at compound interest.

72 ÷ 8% (interest rate) = 9 (years to double investment)

This rule can also dramatically illustrate the importance of just a few percentage points on a long-term investment.

For example:
Assume Sheila Tompkins, age 30, intends to retire at age 65. She invests $10,000 at 8%. Her investment will double just under 4 times during the next 35 years. (4 x 9 = 36). But what if she could earn an average of 10% on the investment?

72 ÷ 10 = 7 (rounded off)

By the time Sheila reaches age 65, her investment will have doubled 5 times (7 x 5 = 35). An increase of only two percentage points in her investment earnings will double her entire retirement fund.

yield a higher rate of return than that paid by traditional, low-risk products. Then, the counselor might explain that investments with some element of risk offer the potential for greater appreciation within a shorter time period. The counselor can mention that many investors are willing to risk some portion of their investment capital in order to secure a greater return. Figure 6-2 shows how different types of investments offer greater potential and demonstrates a ratio of risk to possible return. For example, U.S. government securities and deposit accounts would have a low

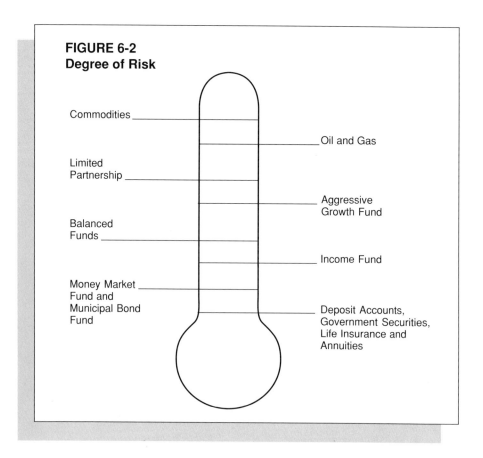

**FIGURE 6-2
Degree of Risk**

Commodities

Oil and Gas

Limited
Partnership

Aggressive
Growth Fund

Balanced
Funds

Income Fund

Money Market
Fund and
Municipal Bond
Fund

Deposit Accounts,
Government Securities,
Life Insurance and
Annuities

risk factor, a municipal bond fund would be higher but still involve minimal risk, an income fund would be higher and an aggressive growth fund would rank higher still (fairly high risk).

Able to Relate Products to Customer Needs and Objectives

As noted above, the essence of consultative selling is matching the institution's products to the individual customer's needs. This is the exact opposite of the "hard-sell" method, in which the salesperson attempts to sell a product only to make a sale without considering whether the product fits the customer's needs and objectives. The consultative approach, in contrast, puts the customer's concerns ahead of the seller's.

Counselors need a range of skills and attitudes in order to relate products to customers' needs and objectives. One of the most important skills is listening—counselors must be able to process both verbal and nonverbal messages from their customers. Closely related to listening skills are questioning skills. The counselor must be able to pose the right questions in order to help the customer to assemble the information needed to make a good decision.

Among the attitudes that a counselor needs to conduct consultative selling is respect for the individual's values. In their work, counselors will encounter a wide range of individuals, each with a unique personal experience. Some of these individuals may hold values similar to those of the counselor, but many of them will have priorities and goals that differ from those of the counselor. The counselor must be able to refrain from judging each individual's goals and values and help each individual to achieve his or her goals.

Responsible to the Customer and the Institution

Interviewing a customer on personal finances places a great deal of responsibility on the counselor. One important concern is confidentiality. The customer must feel assured that his or her privacy will be respected. While many counselors are already aware of this requirement, it has special significance in the context of the products presented in this book. Because these products are intended to address long-term financial concerns, the interview can touch on some sensitive matters.

The counselor must also remember that he or she represents the savings institution to the customer. Financial counseling is most helpful when given with care and discretion. Also, product details are more easily absorbed when described in a clear and understandable manner. The nontraditional products presented in this book can be confusing to the average customer. The savings counselor should bear in mind that his or her description of a mutual fund, annuity or single-premium life policy may represent the customer's first encounter with this type of product.

The savings institution's various prospectuses and brochures on its product offerings provide a wealth of information. Representatives of the brokerage houses and insurance companies that originate these products can be a valuable resource for answering counselors' or customers' questions. The counselor is advised to exercise great caution in discussing these products, particularly when it comes to product guarantees and performance. No customer should ever have grounds for suspecting misrepresentation.

THE SELLING PROCESS

The sale of a product to a customer is the end result of a process; it is not an isolated event that occurs at the counselor's desk. The sale is the final element in a progressive chain of events:

1. initial contact by customer and referral to counselor;

2. the sales interview;

3. follow-up of the sale.

In addition to being vital elements in the selling process, these components are important functions in themselves.

Initial Customer Contact and Referral to Counselor

The customer who appears at the counselor's desk will have been contacted by the institution in one of several ways. The customer may have received a special mailing or come into the counselor's office in response to a media advertisement. Perhaps a teller or some other employee directed an existing accountholder to the representative because that customer requested certain information. Or, the counselor may have arranged the appointment by telephone based on a referral from another customer.

The Sales Interview

Like the sales process outlined above, the actual selling interview entails a series of steps. Each step is important in itself because the outcome of the entire sequence will be a customer decision. Following the process increases the chances of a favorable decision. Downplaying or omitting a step can negatively affect the outcome of the interview.

Before examining the individual steps in a sales interview, note one key point: one of the hallmarks of the professional salesperson is *control*. The institution has demonstrated its confidence in that representative by placing him or her in the position of counseling its customers. The successful counselor is always aware of being the "expert" and the one in charge of the situation. If the counselor allows the interview to wander off the track, the result will be more a casual chat than a professional consultation.

The consultative type of sales interview might be compared to a doctor-patient exchange. The counselor takes down information relevant to the customer's financial needs and objectives. Then the counselor examines and evaluates this information. Finally, the counselor recommends solutions for the problems disclosed during the interview.

The following paragraphs present the key ideas and details of conducting the steps involved in a typical consultative selling interview. Because savings institutions often design their own sales tracks and selling sequences, the discussion avoids specific wording, focusing on general concepts and interview objectives.

Interview Preliminaries: Setting the Stage

It often helps to begin an interview with some general pleasantries, such as the weather, noncontroversial news items or anything that seems appropriate. This helps dissipate any tension. The opening might be followed by some general remarks about how the institution wishes to help customers design personalized savings and investment programs. In closing this preliminary part of the interview, it is often worthwhile to help the customer see the benefits of taking time to plan one's finances. For example, the counselor might say, "You're right in investing this time to make the most out of your money" or "I think you'll see that our services make it easy for you to take charge of your own finances." The counselor might also mention that the institution offers a wide range of products designed to help customers achieve their individual objectives.

Fact Finding and Data Gathering

The fact-finding and data-gathering stage of the sales interview concerns two important objectives. The first involves learning the customer's needs and financial objectives. The second is discovering what the customer has already accomplished in the way of savings and investments.

An informal but purposeful atmosphere is the appropriate setting for this important step of the selling process. A relaxed approach on the counselor's part contributes to a free exchange of information. However, the counselor's mission is to obtain specific information on the customer's assets and goals and determine how to classify the individual's investment preferences. The counselor should ask questions and take notes to make certain that all necessary information is gathered and to make certain that the customer's time is used efficiently. The alert interviewer will discern a pattern that reveals the customer's feelings about investments, including attitudes toward risks and diversification. This knowledge will be helpful when it is time to recommend specific products.

During this stage of the interview, the representative discovers how the customer has handled financial objectives in the past. There may also be an obvious discrepancy between what the customer wants to accomplish and what he or she has done so far. However, the counselor should avoid criticizing the customer's past actions. Any shortcomings in the customer's previous attempts to achieve goals can be brought up later in the discussion, when recommendations are made.

Helping the Customer Prioritize Objectives

Helping the customer prioritize—put first things first—is an essential objective in effective financial counseling. In the course of a selling interview, so many needs and problems may be uncovered that the customer is overwhelmed. If this happens, no decision may be made or action taken, and the whole process will end up a waste of time.

However, the counselor can take steps to help the customer arrange priorities. It is helpful at this point to find out how the customer ranks the relative importance of the listed needs and objectives. Decisions will hinge on such issues as college education funds, downpayments for primary or vacation home purchases, retirement needs and many other factors. One way to start is to list short-term and long-term goals. Once the customer realizes that not all problems need be solved at one time, he or she will be more motivated to work out a realistic financial plan.

Discussing Solutions

At this point in the interview, it is appropriate to discuss some solutions to the problems facing the customer. Here is another opportunity for the representative to demonstrate a sincere interest in the customer's opinions and to reinforce the institution's commitment to serving the customer in a caring, individualized manner.

By this time, the counselor should be able to secure the customer's agreement on an important point: the customer's first investment priority. Perhaps it is setting up an educational fund for a child or an investment that will generate retirement income. Whatever the priority, now is the time for the counselor to present a particular product.

It is beyond the scope of this book to provide detailed steps for this part of the selling process. Each institution has its preferences as to how the counselor presents the product. Further, the insurance company and/or brokerage firm that distributes specific products may suggest the sequence of the steps that will best illustrate the product's points of interest. While each provider of financial services may develop its own procedures for counselors who sell its products, counselors may always make certain that the customer is comfortable with the process. If the customer seems uncomfortable, the counselor should try to learn why. Often, customers may become uncomfortable if they do not understand a point that the counselor presents. Alert counselors watch for signs that customers may not understand the ideas that they are presenting so that these ideas do not become barriers during the interview.

Closing the Sale

Once the product details have been presented, it is time to close the sale—that is, help the customer make a buying decision. Actually, in a properly designed and conducted sales interview, closing takes place throughout the selling process. There is no great mystery in helping a customer make a final purchase decision. The truly professional salesperson possesses no magical technique for closing a sale. The key—if one exists—is to carefully follow a predetermined sequence of steps, such as those outlined above, and to effectively consummate the sale.

As in the entire interview process, the counselor should control the closing phase of the sales interview. The two objectives in the closing phase of the interview are to complete the application and to collect the money that will fund the investment. Many sales are lost when the salesperson ends the discussion or hesitates to secure the transaction by helping the customer with the application and arranging for the customer's money to be transferred properly.

When the other parts of the sales interview have been successful, the counselor can move into the close by beginning to write information on the application form. While the counselor is completing the application, he or she should also determine how the customer wishes the financial transaction to be accomplished. Whether the funds are being drawn from the counselor's institution or another financial intermediary, the counselor should facilitate the transaction. Overall, the counselor should project the image of a resource person, dedicated to helping the customer to achieve his or her financial objectives.

Summary of the Consultative Sales Process

- The representative controls the interview. This is not as formidable a task as it may appear. Customers often appreciate someone who "takes charge" and leads them away from their problems toward a solution.

- It is helpful to summarize needs and objectives and discuss how the customer may have handled solutions to these problems in the past at various points in the interview. This may also point to a discrepancy between the customer's goals and what he or she has actually achieved. The counselor will do better to explain any lack of progress rather than criticize past financial decisions.

- Misunderstandings can be avoided if at various points in the interview the representative checks statements or information that the customer has supplied. This helps ensure that the counselor has understood the information and is on the right track.

- It is important to concentrate on the key issues. If the customer has indicated priorities, the accomplished salesperson will focus on and not digress to other products and solutions.
- It is essential to present product details and key ideas clearly and positively. Customers can get confused if too many ideas are presented in a short time and details are unclear.
- The close should be carried out as a natural part of good customer service.

A well defined sales process such as that presented in this chapter is vitally important to the entire selling process. It helps the counselor project a confident image that in turn helps the customer feel comfortable about making an important financial decision.

Following Up the Sale

To the professional salesperson, the sales process does not end with the closing. The ongoing relationship between the customer and the institution is an asset that is strengthened through ongoing customer service. Furthermore, a good relationship with the customer can mean additional sales opportunities, such as providing for goals and objectives that ranked lower on the customer's priority list. A skillful salesperson will also be able to obtain referrals to other prospective customers from the purchaser, thus creating new customers for the institution.

Selling is a craft and, like all skills, requires a certain amount of study and practice. The savings counselor is in a position that permits on-going learning and constant opportunities to improve his or her selling skills. Each customer presents a unique challenge, giving the representative the opportunity to use different and creative approaches to solving problems.

LICENSING REQUIREMENTS

The selling of two major classifications of products presented in this book—insurance products and mutual funds—is subject to specific licensing requirements. Insurance products—annuities and life insurance—come under state jurisdiction. Licensing examinations are given by state authorities. Mutual funds, being security products, are licensed by the National Association of Securities Dealers. Variable annuities are considered both an insurance product and a security product and therefore require both types of licenses. Individual states may specify additional requirements.

FOOTNOTES

[1]"Tax Deferred Annuity Sales," *Savings Institutions*, Oct. 1987, U.S. League of Savings Institutions.

GLOSSARY

A

accumulation period Period of time during which premiums on an annuity are paid and accumulate with earnings.

accumulation unit Measurement unit expressing the investment value in a variable annuity.

actuary Person trained in the technical aspects of insurance and related areas, such as calculating premiums, reserves and other values.

adhesion Characteristic of a life insurance contract wherein the prospective insured person accepts the company's contract exactly as offered.

aleatory Characteristic of a life insurance contract wherein one party may gain more than the other as a result of a chance occurrence.

annuitant Individual who receives payments from an annuity.

annuity Contract, usually issued by a life insurance company, that provides regular payments either for a designated time period or for life.

annuity unit Measurement unit used in assessing the amount of income a variable annuity yields at maturity; converted from accumulation units.

B

bail-out provision Annuity contract option that allows the owner to avoid a surrender charge when cashing in the contract prematurely; typically exercised after the original guarantee period has expired when the prevailing interest rate falls below a stated percentage of the original rate.

balanced fund Mutual fund that seeks to conserve investors' principal, pay current income and promote long-term growth; generally maintains a portfolio comprised of common stocks, preferred stocks and bonds.

basket (of goods and services) The total of market prices for goods and services that a typical American family might purchase. Used to measure regular changes in the consumer price index. *See also* consumer price index.

beneficiary Person or entity that receives life insurance policy proceeds upon the insured's death; often designated as a *primary beneficiary* (the first to receive benefits) or a *contingent beneficiary* (receives benefits if the primary beneficiary is deceased when proceeds are paid).

Best's Insurance Reports A publication that lists life insurance companies and rates their financial stability. A companion volume, *Best's Flitcraft Compend*, lists insurance companies' product and rate information.

bid price *See* net asset value.

broker/dealer Sales firm that distributes stocks, bonds, mutual funds and other securities directly to the public.

C

capital gain Profit derived from sale of real estate, securities or other capital assets.

capital loss Loss incurred when real estate, securities or other capital assets are sold.

cash refund Annuity option guarantee that returns a lump sum to a beneficiary on funds left on deposit after payments made during the annuitant's lifetime.

cash value Cash build-up in a permanent life insurance policy; may increase by the value of any dividends not previously withdrawn upon surrender of the policy; may or may not equal or exceed the premiums paid in depending on costs of mortality, policy load and other factors.

class beneficiary Beneficiary who is not specifically named; designation indicates the insured's wish to have proceeds divided equally among members of the designated group.

closed-end fund Investment company that issues a specified number of shares, after which purchases must be made in the open market; does not redeem its own shares.

commercial paper Unsecured short-term promissory note issued by a corporation at a discount from face value.

company-managed variable annuity Annuity in which the investment portfolio is fully managed by the insurance company issuing the policy.

conditional Characteristic of a life insurance contract specifying that the insured must meet certain conditions in order to receive proceeds.

consultative selling Type of selling process that ascertains the customer's individual needs and objectives and also considers what the customer already owns before attempting a further sale.

consumer price index (CPI) Economic index prepared by the U.S. Department of Labor that measures continuous changes in the price of a selected group of consumer goods.

contingent beneficiary Beneficiary of a life insurance or annuity contract who receives proceeds if the primary beneficiary is deceased. *See* primary beneficiary.

CREF Acronym for College Retirement Equities Fund; the first variable annuity program.

D

deferred annuity Annuity in which benefit payments begin after a certain number of years following the original purchase.

distribution period Period of time during which annuity benefits are paid out.

diversification Investment strategy that reduces risk by spreading investments over a variety of asset types.

dividend A payment made to a stock or bond purchaser representing a share of profits from the investments. *See also* life insurance dividend.

E

entire contract clause Clause in a life insurance policy stating that the policy and the original application constitute the complete contract.

entry fees A sales charge levied at the purchase date of mutual fund shares. The fee is deducted from the total amount of the purchase and the balance is invested in the fund—also termed a *front-end load*. *See also* exit load.

exit load Sales charge levied when mutual fund shares are sold, called *back-end load*.

expected return Projection of total amount an annuitant will receive upon living to the limit of life expectancy; used to calculate taxable portion of an annuity payment.

extended term insurance *See* paid-up insurance.

F

family of funds Group of mutual funds, each with varying objectives, offered by a brokerage firm; once purchased, the shareholder is free to switch investments among the individual funds, usually without incurring additional sales charges.

fifth dividend option An option wherein the insured may specify that the annual dividend will automatically be used to purchase an additional amount of term insurance; offered in many life insurance policies.

fixed account Investment option in a variable annuity that guarantees safety of principal and a fixed interest rate.

flexible-premium annuity Deferred annuity payments that may be purchased with an optional series of payments offered by the insurance company.

funded Type of underlying investment (i.e. stocks, bonds, money market instruments) that is the financial basis for an annuity or life insurance contract.

G

Ginnie Mae Derived from GNMA (Government National Mortgage Association); securities product composed of pools of federally insured (FHA and VA) mortgages.

grace period   Period (usually 30 or 31 days) during which an overdue premium on an insurance policy may be paid without causing the policy to lapse.

growth fund   Mutual fund with the investment objective of achieving appreciation of capital with little emphasis on dividend income.

I

immediate annuity   Annuity purchased with a single premium in which distribution of benefits begins at the next regularly scheduled payment date following the premium deposit.

income fund   Mutual fund with the investment objective of yielding a high current income.

incontestable clause   Clause in a life insurance contract that designates a time period after which the insurance company may not contest payment of a claim even if there were inaccuracies or misinformation on the original policy application.

inflation   General rise in the prices of goods and services in the economy; often measured in percentage changes in the consumer price index.

installment refund   Annuity option guarantee that offers to return in installments any sum left on deposit after benefits have been paid during annuitant's lifetime.

institutional investor   A corporate investor, such as an educational institution, a union, or group of employers investing in the market usually on behalf of their own pension and/or profit-sharing funds.

interest-only option   Life insurance policy settlement option under which proceeds remain on deposit with the insurance company and only interest is paid out.

Investment Advisers Act of 1940 Legislation that required individuals giving investment advice to register with the Securities and Exchange Commission.

Investment Company Act of 1940 Legislation that brought investment companies under federal control and that provides for registration and regulation of such companies. A major revision in 1970 provided additional amendments concerning management fees and sales charges.

irrevocable beneficiary Beneficiary whose rights cannot be abridged by the policy owner without the beneficiary's consent.

J

joint and survivor annuity Life annuity with two or more annuitants in which payments continue to remaining survivors, in the same or lesser amounts than when the deceased annuitant was living; typical options are joint and one-half and joint and two-thirds.

L

level-premium life insurance Insurance characterized by a premium that remains fixed over the policy's life; in the earlier policy years, there is an overcharge that helps balance the underpayments in later years, when coverage would be more costly.

life annuity Annuity that pays an income to an individual for life with no guarantee periods;

payments cease upon annuitant's death. (Also known as *straight life annuity*.)

life income option   Settlement option in a life insurance contract in which the proceeds may be converted into an annuity.

life insurance dividend   Systematically distributed payment made to the owner of a life insurance policy that largely represents a return of an overcharge of the estimated cost of insurance. *See also* participating policy.

life insurance guaranty fund   A fund composed of contributions from life insurance companies assessed by states in order to guarantee policyholders contract rights in the event a company becomes insolvent.

liquidity   Ease with which an investment can be converted to cash without significant loss.

load fund   Mutual fund in which part of a share's purchase price reflects a sales fee.

M

maturity date   Date at which a life insurance or annuity contract is scheduled to commence payments of the principal sum plus any interest due, including lifetime benefits; term also denotes repayments of principal amounts on securities such as Ginnie Maes and municipal bonds.

money market fund   Mutual fund that invests in short-term money market instruments, such as Treasury bills, commercial paper and certificates of deposits.

mortality table   Statistical table from which insurance companies estimate future deaths per 1,000 from ages 0 to 100; based on information collected on the claim experiences of a group of major life insurance companies.

mutual fund   Open-end investment company composed of a pool of securities that are continually traded according to the individual fund's investment objectives.

N

net asset value (NAV)   (1) Value of a share in an investment company—equals the market value of outstanding securities minus the investment company's liabilities divided by the number of outstanding shares; (2) listed bid price (price at which a mutual fund will redeem its shares).

net cost   The total cost of an investment after sales fees, administrative and investment management fees are included.

no-load fund   Mutual fund that imposes no sales charge for purchase of shares.

nonforfeiture option   Guarantee in a life insurance policy of certain cash or coverage residuals upon termination of premium payments.

nonparticipating policy   Life insurance policy that pays no dividends; typically charges a lower premium than a dividend-paying policy, but eventual net cost may be higher.

O

offering price   Price at which a mutual fund sells its shares to the public—equal to the net asset value (NAV) plus the sales charge if any; also called *asked price*.

open-end fund   Mutual fund that continuously issues shares, creating new shares according to customer demand.

ownership clause   The clause in a life insurance contract that designates all of the contractual rights of the owner of the policy.

P

paid-up insurance   Nonforfeiture life insurance policy option specifying that the policy's original face amount will remain in force for a designated time period, usually called *extended term insurance*.

participating policy   Life insurance policy that pays dividends representing the premium overcharge plus positive experiences on claims, expenses and investment earnings.

period certain   Annuity option that promises to make payments to the beneficiary for a specified number of years regardless of whether the annuitant dies before the end of this period.

permanent insurance   Life insurance coverage in which part of the premium payment is used to establish a savings fund, known as the policy's *cash value*; also known as *whole life* or *straight life*. *See also* level-premium life insurance.

policy owner   Individual named in an annuity or insurance policy who has the authority to exercise all rights in the policy; may or may not be the same person as the insured.

premium   Regular payment made to an insurance company for purchase of an insurance contract.

primary beneficiary   The individual who has prior beneficial rights in collecting life insurance policy proceeds upon the insured's death. *See also* beneficiary.

prospectus Publication that lists pertinent aspects of a securities offering to permit buyers to make informed decisions; according to SEC regulations, must be furnished to a potential buyer before a sale can be executed.

R

redeem Referring to a mutual fund feature in which the fund will readily buy back shares sold to shareholders.

reduced paid-up insurance Nonforfeiture life insurance policy option specifying that a certain amount of life insurance representing a reduction of the original face amount will remain in force, that is, considered as being "paid up."

refund option Option offered in an annuity payment that pays a beneficiary the balance of funds, if any, remaining on deposit after the death of the insured person.

reinstatement clause Clause in a life insurance policy granting the insured the right to reinstate the original coverage in the event of a policy lapse.

renewable term insurance Term insurance that the insured may renew at the end of the policy's life without having to provide further evidence of insurability.

representative In financial planning, an individual licensed to sell a securities product to the public.

return Measurement of investment yield, usually specified as an interest rate.

revocable beneficiary Beneficiary whose status may be revoked by the policy owner without his or her consent or knowledge.

risk   Possibility of loss of principal and/or interest when investing money.

S

saving   Act of retaining a portion of personal income for the purpose of making an investment or a purchase.

Securities Act of 1933   Legislation that specifies that before new corporate securities can be sold, a registration statement containing complete disclosure of the character of the issue must be supplied to the Securities and Exchange Commission and a prospectus filed with that organization.

self-directed variable annuity   Annuity in which the policyholder chooses the investment portfolio from among a family of funds offered by the insurance company.

separate account   Investment pool that funds a variable annuity; invested and administered separately from the insurance company's other investments.

settlement options   Series of choices for receiving life insurance policy proceeds, such as a lump sum cash payment or some form of extended payments.

single-premium whole life   Life insurance policy purchased with a one-time premium; popularly marketed as an investment with income tax advantages.

SIPC   Acronym for Savings Investor Protection Corporation, a government agency that insures investors' accounts for up to $100,000 in the event of the issuing brokerage firm's failure; similar to FSLIC and FDIC insurance.

specific beneficiary   Beneficiary who is specifically named and identified.

spread The profit on an investment made by a savings institution from savers' funds. It is usually the difference between what the institution pays in interest to the customer and the yield that invested funds will earn.

straight life annuity An annuity that will pay income for life but where payments cease upon the death of the annuitant with no remainder for a beneficiary.

suicide clause Provision in a life insurance policy stating that if the insured commits suicide within a specified period (usually one or two years) after purchasing the policy, the death benefit will not be paid and only paid-in premiums will be refunded.

surrender charge A fee charged against the cash value of an insurance or annuity contract when the policy is cashed in at a time designated as premature by the insurance company; similar to an early withdrawal penalty for a certificate of deposit.

surrender value *See* cash value.

T

tax shelter Investment characterized by an income tax incentive; generally involves a higher degree of risk than more conventional investments.

term insurance Life insurance coverage that provides only for death protection; contains no savings element, covers a certain time period and expires at the end of that period.

U

unilateral Characteristic of a life insurance contract specifying that once the insured has paid the premium, only the insurer is liable for a legally enforceable promise during the policy's life.

universal life   Form of flexible-premium, permanent life insurance in which the cash value portion of the policy is separate from the death benefit funding; generally features interest rates competitive with money market and bond yields and permits periodic adjustments in amount of coverage to suit the policy owner's circumstances.

V

valued   Characteristic of a life insurance contract that specifies the amount to be paid in the event of the insured's death.

variable account   A diversified pool of investments designed as a mutual fund to be offered as an option for accumulating funds within a variable annuity.

variable annuity   Annuity that is funded by a portfolio of stock market investments, including stocks, bonds, government securities and other types of fluctuating financial instruments.

W

whole life insurance   An alternate term for permanent life insurance. *See* permanent insurance.

Y

yearly renewable term   A form of term insurance with a premium that increases annually. The insured is guaranteed that the policy may be renewed each year without new medical evidence of insurability.

INDEX